The Bible, Social Media and Digital Culture

This book centres on the use of the Bible within contemporary digital culture and gives an overview of its use online with examples from brand-new research from the CODEC Research Centre at Durham University, UK. It examines the shift from a propositional to a therapeutic approach to faith from a sociological standpoint.

This book explores the ordinary social performance of Bible engagement within digital culture. It explores the data as they relate to Abby Day's concept of performative belief, picking up on Mia Lövheim's challenge to see how this concept works out in digital culture and social media. It also compares the data to various construals of contemporary approaches to faith performative faith, including Christian Smith and Melissa Lundquist Denton's concept of moralistic therapeutic deism. Other research is also compared to the findings of these projects, including a micro-project on Celebrities and the Bible, to give a wider perspective on these issues in both the UK and the USA.

As a sociological exploration of contemporary digital culture and its relationship to sacred texts, this will be of keen interest to scholars of Biblical studies, religion and digital media, and contemporary lived religion.

Peter M. Phillips is Research Fellow in Digital Theology and the Director of the Centre for Digital Theology (formerly CODEC) at Durham University, UK. He has many years of experience teaching and researching the New Testament and now explores the interface between the digital and theological.

Routledge Focus on Religion

Amoris Laetitia and the spirit of Vatican II
The Source of Controversy
Mariusz Biliniewicz

Muslim and Jew
Origins, Growth, Resentment
Aaron W. Hughes

The Bible and Digital Millennials
David G. Ford, Joshua L. Mann and Peter M. Phillips

The Fourth Secularisation
Autonomy of Individual Lifestyles
Luigi Berzano

Narratives of Faith from the Haiti Earthquake
Religion, Natural Hazards and Disaster Response
Roger Philip Abbott and Robert S. White

The Bible, Social Media and Digital Culture
Peter M. Phillips

For more information about this series, please visit: www.routledge.com/Routledge-Focus-on-Religion/book-series/RFR

The Bible, Social Media and Digital Culture

Peter M. Phillips

LONDON AND NEW YORK

First published 2020 by Routledge

2 Park Square, Milton Park, Abingdon, Oxon, OX14 4RN
605 Third Avenue, New York, NY 10017

Routledge is an imprint of the Taylor and Francis Group, an informa business

First issued in paperback 2020

Copyright © 2020 Peter M. Phillips

The right of Peter M. Phillips to be identified as author of this work has been asserted by him in accordance with sections 77 and 78 of the Copyright, Designs and Patents Act 1988.

All rights reserved. No part of this book may be reprinted or reproduced or utilised in any form or by any electronic, mechanical, or other means, now known or hereafter invented, including photocopying and recording, or in any information storage or retrieval system, without permission in writing from the publishers.

Notice:
Product or corporate names may be trademarks or registered trademarks, and are used only for identification and explanation without intent to infringe.

British Library Cataloguing-in-Publication Data
A catalogue record for this book is available from the British Library

Library of Congress Cataloging-in-Publication Data
A catalog record for this book has been requested

ISBN: 978-0-367-02877-0 (hbk)
ISBN: 978-0-367-78792-9 (pbk)

Typeset in Times New Roman
by Apex CoVantage, LLC

Contents

List of figures vi
List of tables vii

Introduction 1

1 The contemporary context of Bible engagement, especially in the UK and USA 6

2 The Bible, social media and digital culture 20

3 Popular Bible verses on social media 35

4 Analysis/reflection 64

5 Some potential contributory factors: performative belief, MTD and media ecology 91

Conclusion: an ordinary canon within social media engagement? 111

References 114
Index 125

Figures

3.1	Frequency of Bible verses in print culture	41
4.1	BGP13–18, verse frequency	74
4.2	Google Trends, NIV translations for Jeremiah 29:11, John 3:16, Philippians 4:13	87
4.3	Google Trends, Jeremiah 29:11 (NIV), John 3:16 (NIV), Philippians 4:13 (KJV)	89

Tables

3.1	*YouVersion* statistics from 2013–2018	43
3.2	Web engagement statistics from the Barna Group	44
3.3	The aggregate list	61
4.1	YVP13–18	65
4.2	BGP13–18	73
4.3	BGP13–18	77

Introduction

In *Believing in Belonging*, Abby Day (2011) challenged the use of surveys and censuses within contemporary sociology of religion studies. She argued that it was not possible to determine whether someone who said they were a Christian in a survey actually practiced, or performed, that religion. To some extent, her book challenges Grace Davie's book *Religion in Britain Since 1945* (Davie, 1994), in which she had argued that church decline was part of a process of people believing without belonging.

Day works from a Durkheimian emphasis on the performance of belief:

> Durkheim's well-known definition of religion as "a unified system of beliefs and practices relative to sacred things takes propositional belief as a starting point but moves it into the realm of performance.
>
> (Day, 2011, p. 10)

But whereas Durkheim's focus was on the performance of the Church and society, Day wants to focus on the 'embodied, emotional experience of belonging' (Day, 2011, p. 10), picking up themes from Mary Douglas, among others, to argue that belief arises not from creeds but "as a pragmatic (I would add 'performative') means for a 'believer' to impose order and achieve a sense of coherence" (Day, 2011, p. 13). As such, Day wants to "illustrate how and why people today in Euro American modern societies construct, negotiate, and perform beliefs" (Day, 2011, p. 27).

In a slightly earlier article (Day, 2010), Day herself linked her understanding more to the issue about propositional belief, which she proposed undergirded Davie's 'believing without belonging' concept. She argued that the decline in church attendance was because believers were "moving from propositional forms of belief to a practice-centred view of belief" (Day, 2010, p. 11). In other words, people might say they believed this or that proposition, but their belief was seen much more clearly in how they lived out their beliefs in their daily lives. Making use of Durkheim's

2 *Introduction*

understanding of religion as social function, she argues that in fact belief is performative – "no longer timeless or universal" but part of the socialization of the performer (2010, p. 14). As with social networks, people engage in homophily – speaking and sharing with like-minded people in like-minded ways – or as Day argues: "it brings into being a social reality for the informant and provides a sense of cultural homogeneity" (Day, 2011, p. 49). The issue is less about propositional belief (see James Beckford in Cotter, 2016, pp. 102–103) than it is about performative belief (2010, p. 17), about living out beliefs within a wider social context:

> I have suggested here that performative belief is one way of describing how beliefs are acted and help shape identities. Belief is not separate from identity or social context but a way of creating who 'I' am relative to 'you' here and now. Through the quality of emotion and corporeal experience in human relationships, performative belief is how people can adjust to given social contexts, expectations and aspirations.
> (Day, 2010, p. 26)

In response to extensive fieldwork, Day develops her 'seven dimensions of belief' model: content, sources, practice, salience, function, place and time" (Day, 2011, pp. 158–173). Using this model, Day proposed that the phenomenon of non-religious people bringing into being a Christian identity related to social belongings is best explored by the concept of "performative Christianity" (Day, 2011, p. 192). "Doing belief', then, says Day, "is described as an active, reflective orientation towards belief arising from human, emotional interaction and personal reflection" (Day, 2011, p. 193). 'Performative belief' is a construct within which "belief is not pre-formed but a lived, embodied performance" (Day, 2011, p. 194). For Day, such belief is in the social reality or construct of belonging. One might ask whether there is a sense of belonging which might also be focussed on belief.

In 2016, a number of sociologists were brought together to comment on Day's work (Cotter, 2016). In this article, Beckford summarized Day's three key points (Cotter, 2016, p. 102):

- "People 'perform' beliefs in different ways in different places and times as strategies for adapting their identity to perceived circumstances"
- Such 'performative belief' helps people feel socially connected with people with whom they feel they belong
- This sense of belonging does not necessarily end with their death

While accepting much of Day's argument, Mia Lövheim raises some interesting questions about how Day's theory of performative belief might be worked out within an increasingly mediatized understanding of religion. Lövheim is more than happy with Day's "core arguments about belief as affective, embodied, and performed and the need to relocate belief from the individual to the social, from the transcendent to the mundane" (Lövheim in Cotter, 2016, pp. 106–108). But she presses the argument further by picking up Day's seven-dimensional model of belief (Day, 2011, p. 155), arguing:

> This model shows how the content of belief becomes meaningful only in relation to how beliefs are practiced and felt in social relations and fundamentally shaped by the material, social, and historical conditions in which people live their daily lives.
> (Lövheim in Cotter, 2016, p. 107)

Lövheim then links this to the ongoing process of the mediatization of religion, which includes "not only technical devices but also social and cultural contexts for the construction of meaning, values, and identity". Indeed, she argues that religion per se does not have an essence but rather "emerges through mediation between known and visible human values and unknown and invisible 'transcendent' values" (Cotter, 2016, p. 107). Picking up the focus on ethnographic research in Day's work, Lövheim asks what it would mean to look for performative belief in the digital world where close relationships are mediated through e-mail, Skype, text messages and social network sites such as Facebook and YouTube?

To some extent Lövheim's challenge had already been met in the work of Heidi Campbell (2005, 2010, 2013), Heidi Campbell and Stephen Garner (2016) and Pauline Hope Cheong (2012, 2013, 2014, 2016) in their explorations of the impact of media technology on Christian community and especially in Campbell's exploration of the social shaping of technology. Moreover, a recent edited collection of digital methodologies captures various glimpses of this work across different religious communities (Cheruvallil-Contractor and Shakkour, 2015), with a helpful reminder in a new collection of essays on Digital Ethnography (Pink et al., 2016) that the focus needs to be on social performance and not on the digital gadgets. In fact, the work goes wider because of Day's own call for a study of performative belief to "be relocated from the individual to the social, from the transcendent to the mundane" (Day, 2011, p. 6). Performative belief is practiced in the everyday, where in digital culture social media provides a script of life, the phatic communication (see Chapter 3), the background music to life. A kind of belief of the everyday which harks back to Michel de Certeau's work on scripted lives (de Certeau, 1984). Such concepts fit well into Jeff Astley's concept of 'ordinary theology' (2001, 2014) – "the content, pattern and processes of ordinary people's articulation of their religious understanding" (Astley, 2001, 56).

4 *Introduction*

Day's exploration of the movement from propositional belief to performative belief will also be picked up in what follows, especially in terms of the proposed shift towards a belief which works, which is lived out in the life of the believer. (2010, p. 11). To some extent, this is reminiscent of the wider shift which George Lindbeck calls the shift from 'propositional' to 'experiential' expressions of faith (Lindbeck, 2002, pp. 169–195), or which Davie calls a shift from formal to informal religion (Davie, 2000, pp. 176–194), or Stephen Heelas and Linda Woodhead refer to as 'the spiritual turn' (Heelas and Woodhead, 2005). In the USA, Christian Smith and Melinda Lundquist Denton (2005) have proposed a construal of religion, based on a large survey and in depth interviews with American young people as 'moralistic therapeutic deism' – a construal which specifically notes the shift from a propositional to a therapeutic approach to faith – from 'I believe that' to a practical faith which fits a therapeutic agenda.

This is the milieu of this little book – I am running with Day's sense of performative belief but also taking up Lövheim's challenge to explore social media to see how the ordinary social performance of Bible engagement within digital culture affects how the Bible is portrayed online and what verses are most popular in that social media engagement.

So this book is all about the *ordinary social performance* of Bible engagement within digital culture.

- *Ordinary* in terms of Astley uses the term to talk about everyday expressions of faith. Indeed, it may go beyond Astley who is very centred on the church-goer. Here 'ordinary' tends to mean 'everyday'. With lists drawn from billions of data entries and hundreds of millions of unique users across every continent, the lists do provide perhaps the closest we can get to ordinary social performance of Bible engagement in the contemporary world – ordinary people engaging with the Bible.
- *Social performance* of Bible engagement because whenever people highlight, bookmark or share a Bible verse within social media they are creating a social performance – something which reveals something about their own identity and also something about their own perceived audience. It's a performance about their beliefs about themselves, their audiences and the Bible. They are performing their belief. Perhaps for themselves. Perhaps for others. They may be evangelizing their audience – this is the Bible reading you need to read to make you a better person. They may be offering guidance – follow this and you will be well. They may be offering judgement – do this or else. Or they may simply be offering to the wider world something which they themselves have found in some way beautiful, touching, healing.

In Chapter 1, I will set the scene and explore Bible Engagement in contemporary society – especially in the UK and USA.

In Chapter 2, I look at the performative aspects of social media engagement, exploring some of the more theoretical aspects about social media interactions and how the user often has difficulty working out precisely whom they are addressing and how they compensate for social media's context collapse. The chapter will also offer a brief overview of the literature on the Bible in the digital age.

In Chapter 3, I provide the core lists which I am exploring in this book – 20 lists from a range of organizations between 2012 and 2019 offering popular Bible verses in various forms of social media engagement.

In Chapter 4, I offer some interpretation and reflection on these lists, picking up the themes of performative belief.

In Chapter 5, I take a more detailed look at the shift towards performative belief, especially in terms of Smith and Denton's *Soul Searching* (2005).

In the Conclusion, I sum up my findings and ask whether social media is transforming both the online image and canon of the Bible.

1 The contemporary context of Bible engagement, especially in the UK and USA

The Bible has surely been one of the most iconic texts of any civilization. It stands alongside the greatest examples of world literature. Its existence and its use has changed the course of civilizations. An almost epic description of the Bible was once penned by Frank McConnell (1986, p. 4) and has been retold by scholars since:[1]

> The book has become an equivalent, in its sheer existence, to the salvation of the soul or of the people. This is a cultural phenomenon of the most cataclysmic order. . . . No book has exercised a stronger influence upon the whole course of Western writing. . . . And no book has been less a book and more a living entity in the evolving consciousness of [the West].

McConnell's bigger point concerns the historical importance of sacred texts in general but especially of the Bible: they became epoch-changing, civilization-shaping phenomena. They become so much more than the sum of their parts. They become transcendent texts. It's a kind of bibliocentrism – where the Bible becomes a core element of a culture, the foundational text. McConnell's bibliocentricism stands for the West, for Christendom, but different cultures have different classics. As Homer offered a mythology, morality and transcendence for Ancient Greece, as Virgil's *Aeneid* offered an epic identity for Rome in transition from Republic to Empire, so the two Testaments of the Bible arguably offered a new retelling of mythology, morality and transcendence for Christendom (Alexander, 2006). T.S. Eliot, in discussing the nature of a 'classic text' (1956, pp. 53–71), argues that the production of a classic text focusses subsequent literary attention on that classic – that future literature is a retelling or a renewal or an echo of the skill or artistry of that classic. The classic becomes universal and transcends the context and specificity of its origins.

The Bible resourced Christendom. It provided the moral, judicial and, often, repressive agenda for Western civilization. But it has also been (and continues to be?) an inspiration for the arts and creative industries. Biblical themes and tropes are scattered liberally through our culture in verse, prose, song, in paintings, films and ads. Indeed, the structures of Christendom and the reproduction and dissemination of the Bible through the monasteries provided one route to preserve Greco-Roman learning into the pre-modern era. The Bible, in these times, was still an inspiration to literature, art and creativity – as we see in the development of Gospels and Bibles as an art form from Kells to Lindisfarne and throughout the Christian world. Art, architecture, music and literature testify to the Bible's central place at the heart of European culture, as well as in North Africa and Central Asia.

At the same time, most people could not have read the text. Despite recent research into the possibility of an education project within the early Church to ensure more and more people could read the Bible, most people across the years have heard the Bible or seen the Bible rather than read the Bible (Wright, 2017). Although Augustine may have been able to respond to the girl's cry: "*Tolle, lege*" ("Take up and read"), there is no suggestion that for the vast bulk of the population for hundreds of years before or after him such a command would have made any sense at all. Global literacy rates are now good and improving further – and ironically in this era of literacy, the Bible is engaged with less and less.

Having said that, throughout the medieval period, more and more of the mercantile urban middle class were becoming literate – not least through the influence of guilds who taught their apprentices to read – by an age-old process of literacy being taught through engagement with the Bible dating back at least to Augustine, if not earlier. As such, the monopoly of the elite to determine the meaning of the text was beginning to be deconstructed by both non-literate engagement with the Bible and by ever increasingly Biblical literacy. This literacy created both the urgent need for the printing press as well as its main source of custom. Moreover, this literacy is part and parcel of the movement towards the translation of the Bible into the vernacular and the sowing of social discontent through the Lollards and Anabaptist sects.

Jeffrey Siker (2017, p. ix) opens up his book, *Liquid Scripture*, by citing a famous Johannes Gutenberg quotation taken from the work of Alphonse de Lamartine (1854, vol. 2, p. 287) – a politician/poet/writer in the mid 19th century. The quotation, which does not seem to pre-exist Lamartine, makes some bold assertions about the new press:

> Yes, it is a press, certainly, but a press from which will soon flow in exhaustible streams the most abundant and most marvellous liquor that

has ever flowed to relieve the thirst of men . . . like a new star it will scatter the darkness of ignorance and cause a light heretofore unknown to shine amongst men.

(de Lamartine, 1854, vol. 2, p. 287)

We might compare this to McConnell's bibliocentricity or to Eliot's concept of the classic becoming the central focus of subsequent literature. Did Gutenberg's press provide a paradigm shift moment when suddenly the Bible became more available, more open, more popular? Certainly, the presses printed (and still print) many Bibles and many books about the Bible. But Christianity and the Bible have always been about much more than the book. Over the centuries the vast majority of Christians have heard the text rather than actually read it. In his reflections on Bible engagement in medieval Europe, Eyal Poleg (2013) talks of Bible mediation rather than Biblical literacy, focussing not so much on reading the Bible, but rather on the mediation of the Bible through liturgical processions, sermons and on the Bible as a talisman. He could have looked as well at music, poetry, art, architecture, literature, mystery plays and festivals.

The Bible, its translation into the vernacular and its distribution through the presses – all this was the desire of the reformers. But the Reformation also offers a good example of how the establishment (the Church) seized control of both the book and its interpretation (Poleg, 2013; Ferrell, 2008; Price and Ryrie, 2004). The reformers' zeal to get the Bible into the hands of the common people was always challenged by the establishment. Erasmus himself argued that all people could become theologians by studying the text more, by encountering the text of the Bible itself: "It casts aside no age, no sex, no fortune or position in life. The sun itself is not as common and accessible to all as Christ's teaching" (Erasmus, 1516, as cited in Olin, 1987, p. 101). Indeed, Erasmus goes on to argue that all need access to the text: "Christ wishes his mysteries published as openly as possible . . . even [for] the lowliest women . . . understood not only by the Scots and Irish but also by Turks and Saracens" (ibid.).

Despite his opening rhetoric in the *Paraclesis* about universal literacy, Erasmus does not paint a picture of everyone sitting in Cambridge colleges editing Greek manuscripts. His vision is egalitarian and democratic: all can engage with his Bible. But as an important part of creating a scientific, rational approach to textual criticism and interpretation, Erasmus was part of a process of objectifying the text, of making the text a passive object to be ornamented and revered and then studied and dissected: the Bible became like a patient on an operating table waiting for the skilled surgeon to make it better or to perform an autopsy.

In such conditions, the Bible has increasingly become a closed text to many because of the increasing complexity of the hermeneutical process. Better to let the experts engage and leave the Bible to Sunday services than to try to engage with it from our own relative inexperience. So, Clive Field talks of the Bible as a closed text (Field, 2014) and remarks on the ideological shift away from the Bible as a text of authority and identity for our contemporary culture.

But did that shift start with the Reformation itself? Some might argue that there is an inherent contradiction in the reformers' work. On the one hand, they speak of farmers singing songs, weavers humming psalms, travellers telling stories – of a mediated Bible as part of everyday culture (Poleg, 2013; Price and Ryrie, 2004). Indeed, it is this same Erasmus who will publish his own *Paraphrases*, ready-made sermon guides meant to bring the Bible alive to those who cannot read it. At the same time, the message had to be guarded by special people, usually European white male clerics. Indeed, whenever the Bible has found its own way out, leaking surreptitiously into public and private discourse, the Church and the establishment have often reacted disastrously. The Bible 'in the wild' seems to be a dangerous thing – whether it is the mysticism of Meister Eckhart and Hildegard of Bingen (or, now, the gracious inclusivism of Rachel Held Evans), medieval movements to translate the Bible into English, the diverse tensions within Protestantism, the revolutionary liberation movements in South America in the 20th century, or the rise of Asian and African Exegesis in the 21st.

Of course, the *mediated presence* of the Bible in contemporary societies goes without saying – but that presence is different in the Global South to the Global North, different in secularized Europe and globalized London (Davie, 2017), different in Brexit Britain from Trump's America (Theissen, 2007; Bauckham, 2003; Bielo, 2009; Berlinerblau, 2008). In both the USA and Britain, most homes have a Bible (Field, 2014; American Bible Society, 2018) – but that Bible will, more often than not, stand on the shelf gathering dust. In both societies, the Bible is largely unread and the majority of people (54% in the USA, more in the UK) are disengaged from it as an actual text. It is both a reminder of days gone by, as well as almost a sacred presence within the home: a talisman (Phillips, 2018). Despite this, as we will see next, even as a talisman, the Bible remains important and, at times, authoritative: it is a voice to be brought out in important moments and to attract certain voters (Berlinerblau, 2008; Crossley, 2011; Goff, Farnsley and Thuesen, 2017).

When exploring culturally embedded Biblical literacy in *Rethinking Biblical Literac*y,, Matthew Collins comments: "Rumours of the Bible's 'loss' to modern society are greatly exaggerated. It may no longer play such an

10 *The contemporary context of Bible engagement*

explicitly prominent role in daily life, yet nevertheless continues to saturate our culture and heritage" (Edwards, 2015, p. 90). But that presence, which, in different ways, George Aichele (2001), Yvonne Sherwood (2000), Chris Meredith and Robert Myles (both in Edwards, 2015) refer to as 'afterlives' of the Bible, tends to focus on the transtemporal, transcultural effect of the text and on the cultural reception of the text in contemporary society. Such reception is a reflexive process. So, Aichele explores the concept of the Bible as a classic text, highlighting Eliot's argument that classic texts have afterlives in which they become universal in terms of both space and time (Aichele, 2001, pp. 87–90). Aichele had already asserted that any reading of a classic – a canonical text – changes the essence or intertextuality of both the contemporary receptive reading and our understanding of the target text as well, thus making the classic itself the focus of future creativity, recasting it through echoes, imitations, allusions or parodies (Aichele, 2001, pp. 15–30; Eliot, 1956, pp. 63–65; Genette, 1997). Similarly, Yvonne Sherwood talks of how the book of Jonah survives its own potential demise through cultural re-appropriation – the book lives on within the very readings which seek to unpick it, poison it, drown it. She reminds us of Hugh Pyper's exploration of the Bible as the memeplex, forcing itself upon its readership (Sherwood, 2000, pp. 176–209; Genette, 1997; Pyper in Exum and Moore, 1998; Stahlberg, 2008, pp. 18–37). Similarly, Chris Meredith explores how Eddie Izzard's comic portrayal of the Flood narrative plays on both the audience's knowledge of the Bible as an authoritative text as well as on their sense of awkwardness about mocking that 'classic' text (Meredith in Edwards, 2015, p. 194). Meanwhile, Robert Myles puts cultural reception at the heart of literacy, while reminding us (*contra* Eliot, Aichele and Sherwood) that: "afterlives of the Bible in popular culture typically remove the text from canonical control altogether" (Myles in Edwards, 2015, p. 146).

The work of Poleg (2013) and the authors of *Rethinking Biblical Literacy* (Edwards, 2015) take us away from the Protestant/Enlightenment love affair with 'the word' [of God] (logocentrism or even phallologocentricism) and instead remind us of the very material, sensual, visual elements of both the Bible and of Christian practice in its many forms and many versions. It explores the Bible as a fundamentally mediated text which remains at the heart of contemporary Western culture – the classic which so much creativity seeks to query, challenge, replace, but through such engagement that same creativity actually reinforces the text's status as a classic within contemporary culture.

In focusing more on the 'cultural reception of the Bible' than on 'Bible reading', then, it can be argued, as Collins asserted, that Biblical literacy is not in decline, especially when we see the Bible still as a mediated text. Films, songs, theatre, art, sculpture – even architecture and advertising – carry echoes, afterlives of the Bible. I am reminded of Lady Gaga's constant

The contemporary context of Bible engagement 11

twisting of Biblical imagery (Gellel, 2013), of David Bowie's *Lazarus* (Phillips, 2016), of Darren Aronofsky's *Noah* – a film he referred to as the most unbiblical Biblical epic ever (Phillips, in press). Even playful rebellion against the Bible, in parody or in vitriol, seen from the mystery plays to Monty Python and Izzard, somehow works to reinforce the power that the Bible has within our society. Brian Malley (in Bielo, 2009), whose work I will discuss later, reminds us of this association of 'the Bible' with the wider concept of 'authoritative discourse'.

The question is whether as Christendom crumbles this culturally embedded, mediated Bible, this 'Bible' in concept, will also crumble/dissipate, overtaken by different cultural texts. Just as Eliot's arguments for 'the classic' seem widely divergent from contemporary literary theory, McConnell's passion for the Bible's importance to Western civilization has to be held in tension with the findings of academic research which demonstrate how little the Bible is known or respected among contemporary society (Wochlin, 2005; Field, 2014; Goff et al., 2017). In post-Christendom, the Bible's influence and relevance as a classic seem to be waning, with an increasing sense that people are unaware of the Bible even when it the source for regular phrases people use everyday (Field, 2011). In more recent research carried out by the CODEC Research Centre at Durham University, in partnership with the Bible Society, we found that most Digital Millennials (18-to 34-year-olds who regularly use digital technology) were pretty indifferent to the Bible. They acknowledged its presence, even tending to call it the 'word of God', and they would show some unease when people seemed to be laughing at it – but overall the situation was one of qualified indifference. The Bible was not part of their own world or their experience (Ford, Mann and Phillips, 2019).

More widely, in 2014, Field published an article exploring all the evidence from British opinion polling about the Bible from the 1940s to 2013 (Field, 2014). Field argues not that Biblical literacy per se is in decline but rather that Bible-centricism is on the way out. The research is not so much about how often people read the Bible, but rather how people are losing the quality of 'Bible-centricism', which itself acts as a portmanteau term that includes Bible ownership, regular Bible reading, Bible knowledge, and belief in the Bible's veracity and its influence in everyday life. As such, Field is looking for a pretty elite form of Biblical literacy and engagement, which he thinks should at least still be present within the Church.

The data for Field's research consist of 123 broadly representative opinion polls, alongside 35 polls of adult religious populations. Field found overall that household Bible ownership has slumped (from 90% to around 67%); weekly Bible reading, never high, has fallen from around 16% to 9%; about 77% of the population rarely reads the Bible or has never read the Bible; and knowledge about the Bible has also fallen. He also finds that Bible belief has waned to such an extent that

> only a small and dwindling minority believes the Bible to be true. . . . Key storylines in the Bible – Creation, Virgin Birth, gospel miracles, Resurrection – have been progressively rejected as historically inaccurate and/or understood in a figurative sense or disbelieved entirely.
> (Field, 2014, 517)

Significantly, as CODEC found with the Digital Millennials, for around half of all adults surveyed between 2008 and 2011, the Bible has "absolutely no significance in their personal lives" (Field, 2014, 516). Field's article is almost apocalyptic in tone, making the point that the Bible was not written to be "the moral framework of Judeo-Christian civil societies" but rather is meant to be "the cornerstone of the Christian faith, at once its inspiration, authority and evidential basis" (Field, 2014, 503).

We have already seen that there are alternative voices which are less apocalyptic. *Rethinking Biblical Literacy* (Edwards, 2015) contains numerous essays pointing to the persistence of a (mediated) Bible within contemporary society. Others have pointed out that the Bible assumed within contemporary British society is a 'decaffeinated' text, a text which fails to explore the radical edge of the Bible as well as some of the problematic teachings of the Bible for contemporary progressive societies. So, James Crossley (2011, p. 209) talks of the Bible assumed by contemporary society as reinforcing Western liberal capitalism: "a text of liberty, freedom, democracy, gender equality, and everything it is not".

Field's statistics and general anecdotal evidence show a clear decline in Bible literacy and engagement in the UK, despite ongoing representations of Biblical imagery within contemporary culture (*contra* Edwards, 2015). There are other possible explanations. The (continued) mediated presence of the Bible may represent (potentially diminishing) afterlives of the Bible, echoes of the Bible's long-term status as an authoritative text within Western society. Or that same presence could perhaps point towards the (resurgent) globalized nature of contemporary British society and the (increasing) importance of cultural influences from global communities which have retained a more profound engagement with the Bible text – be that in the plethora of African, Asian and European indigenous churches flourishing in globalized London or in the cultural products of the American-dominated entertainment culture (Davie, 2017; Ford et al., 2019).

Christianity in the USA is, of course, a different kind of thing (for example: Gorski, 2010, 2017a, 2017b) and American Bible engagement remains considerably more robust than in the UK (American Bible Society, 2018;

Goff et al., 2017; Bielo, 2009; Noll, 2015). In their annual report, the American Bible Society notes that Bible ownership is around 82% with about 50% of all Americans considered to be 'Bible-users' – a figure which has remained consistent throughout the annual reports the Society has provided since 2011 (American Bible Society, 2018, p. 8). Having said that, more than half of Digital Millennials are either neutral towards the Bible or disengaged with it – a figure reflected in CODEC's survey of British millennials (Ford et al., 2019). But in the American polling, there is much less sense of decline or abandonment when compared with data presented by Field (2014) for the UK. Bible engagement in the USA is more robust – although, just as in the UK context, there remains a hint that people regard the Bible as an artefact rather than a text to be read. According to the report, 82% own a Bible, but being a 'Bible-user' means reading the Bible only three or four times a year (American Bible Society, 2018, p. 8). The most Bible-centric group represent about 9% of the population, more often than not are married men in their 50s, attend (a Protestant) church regularly and live in the Southern States – 80% of this group read the Bible daily. More than half of the population are categorized as 'Bible disengaged' – indifferent to the Bible although without a sense of hostility to it. There is something here about the Bible as token, symbol and sign rather than the Bible as a well-read text. I will explore this as I look a bit deeper into American engagement with the Bible.

Of course, the second decade of the 21st century has seen a resurgence in the potential influence of Evangelical Christianity in the USA around the election of Donald Trump (Barrett-Fox, 2018). Of course, many evangelicals do not support Trump and the use of the shorthand 'Evangelical Christianity' is itself problematic (Keener, 2017). So, Jacques Berlinerblau (2008) precedes his discussion of the role of the Bible in presidential politics by discussing the place of the Bible more generally in American politics prior to Trump. He begins by recounting a story in which a senior professor ends an argument by declaring: "The Bible is just raw power!" The professor's point was that the Bible can be used, powerfully, on opposing sides of many arguments – it is raw power rather than directed power (Berlinerblau, 2008, p. 4). So, Berlinerblau argues, different sections of society and the Church have employed the Bible passionately in the culture wars in which so many are currently engaged, not least around gender and same-sex relationships and the struggle between progressive liberalism and protectionism (Rodman in Bielo, 2009, 100–113).

Berlinerblau (2008) outlines both the turn towards secularization and the subsequent reverse turn away from secularization at the second half of the 20th century, focussing on the return of the Bible to the political stage in the USA with the election of Ronald Reagan, and the use of the Bible subsequently on both sides of the political divide, especially by

President George W Bush and Barak Obama. Despite sometimes sophisticated engagement in the Bible, especially by Obama, it is the concept of 'Bible' as 'authoritative discourse' (see Malley in Bielo, 2009) and the outworking of that concept that allows both sides of the political debate to argue for a Biblical mandate for their (opposing) views and policies. Berlinerblau's historical review of American Bible engagement frequently notes the use of the Bible to justify different views, or to be used as an icon of religious national identity rather than for the Bible to be engaged specifically: it's as if the Bible and the American way of life fuse into each other. So, he points to the wide use of the Bible within the Revolutionary Congress, despite the fact that few of the revolutionary fathers held what Field would now call a bibliocentric view. Thomas Jefferson, after all, created his own cut-and-pasted Gospels to sift wheat from the chaff (Berlinerblau, 2008, p. 7).

The Bible then seems at times to have operated as a kind of talisman or icon within American culture: honoured publicly but with little actual engagement in politics. It isn't mentioned in the Declaration of Independence or the Constitution. Indeed, the separation of Church and State meant to limit the power of the state to control religion could be seen to deny the Bible the very power which the early Puritan settlers had come to America to establish. Honoured in public but disregarded in politics and civil society, which were to be protected an increasingly buttressed and weaponized separation wall (Berlinerblau, 2008, p. 9; Gorski, 2017b). Of course, Martin Luther King Jr. and the fight for racial justice show a stark alternative to this rather white, male picture (Selby, 2008; Powery in Goff et al., 2017; Wimbush, 2012)!

It is debatable whether the more recent return of 'the Bible' as authoritative discourse underlies the election of Trump in 2016 in any meaningful way (Whitehead, Perry and Baker, 2018; Gorski, 2017a). The political shift among some evangelicals does not obviously relate to actual readings of the text, but rather to a greater focus on what Philip Gorski calls 'Christian nationalism', which includes the concept of 'the Bible' as underpinning the concept of the USA as a Christian nation (Gorski, 2017a). 'Christian nationalism', argues Andrew Whitehead and his colleagues, starts out with civil religion's reference to "America's covenant relationship with a divine Creator who promises blessings for fulfilling its responsibility to defend liberty and justice", but then focusses much more on Hebrew Bible parallels between the USA and Israel and the "command to maintain cultural and blood purity, often through war, conquest and separatism" (Whitehead et al., 2018, p. 150). In contrast, civil religion seems to reflect Berlinerblau's exegesis of American culture during the secularization period prior to the evangelical resurgence with a noticeable split between propositional belief in Christianity/the Bible but an adherence to the social concept of the Christian nation.

The contemporary context of Bible engagement 15

But how does all of this impact on American Bible engagement? In the conclusion to his reflections on Bible engagement around presidential politics, Berlinerblau (2008, p. 133) concedes that the Bible is indeed back. But his following sentence is telling: "And it is as somewhat relevant as ever". In other words, the Bible in American society remains as an icon or talisman reminding (some) Americans of their destiny to defend liberty and justice and urging (other) Americans to re-assert Christian nationalism through all means available. It's a performance of 'the Bible' as concept rather than an engaged reading of the Biblical text.

This same ambivalence about the role of the Bible within American society is evidenced in *The Bible in American Life* (Goff et al., 2017), the report of a Lilley-funded three-year research project based at Indiana University–Purdue University Indianapolis (IUPUI). So, in his retrospective exploration of the Bible in the USA, Mark Noll opens with the sentence: "The Bible remains nearly ubiquitous in American public life" (Noll in Goff et al., 2017, p. 331). His argument reflects *Rethinking Biblical Literacy*'s insistence that cultural Biblical literacy is alive and kicking (Noll in Goff et al., 2017, p. 331; compare Edwards, 2015, p. ix–x): "Wherever you care to look, examples abound-on the internet, in the movies, on television, in bookstores, in public rhetoric, in the names of people and places, and (not least) in political conflict keyed to the nation's culture wars". However, after a catalogue of the Bible's star appearances throughout American culture both offline and online, Noll does concede that the citation of the Bible in everyday public rhetoric has decreased, and that where it is cited, there is often an equal and opposite argument citing alternative Bible verses – the same sense of dissonance about Biblical content which Berlinerblau had noted.

When Noll turns to the statistics of the research, that research points to a gradual decline in Bible engagement and a retrenchment of Bible reading into older age groups, the less educated and the more Southern. One of the clearest findings is associated with race:

> Specifically, [people of colour] read the Bible at a higher rate than people of other races, and by a considerable margin. . . . 70% of all [people of colour] said they read the Bible outside of worship at least once in the past year, compared to 44% of whites [and] 46% for Hispanics.
> (Noll in Goff et al., 2017, p. 339)

The conclusion remains that statistically Bible engagement continues its slow but steady decline in the USA.

Interestingly, Noll concludes his reflection (in Goff et al., 2017, pp. 342–344) by looking at why people in the USA consult the Bible: for prayer and personal devotion, to learn about religion and personal relationship decisions and about health and healing. I will need to pick this up later in my exploration of the motivation behind Bible verses shared on social media, but it does tend to reflect, again, Day's sense of performative engagement with belief. I am interested in how we construct narratives around our identity rather than in exploring particular propositional beliefs – something which I have seen throughout my consideration of American engagement with the Bible.

The introduction to the volume raises similar issues:

> There is a paradox in American Christianity. According to Gallup, nearly eight in ten Americans regard the Bible as either the literal word of God or as inspired by God. At the same time, surveys have revealed – and recent books have analysed – surprising gaps in Americans' Biblical literacy. These discrepancies reveal American Christians' complex relationship with Holy Writ, a subject which is widely acknowledged but rarely investigated.
>
> (Goff et al., 2017, p. xix)

We have already seen that the Bible is an iconic presence within American culture. As Paul Gutjahr (in Goff et al., 2017, p. 8) comments: "There is a separation here between belief and practice ... the Bible takes on a sort of sacred totemic value that might be less instrumental in terms of reading practices than one might originally think". So, Bible reading rates in the USA remain higher than in the UK. Indeed, when considering more habitual reading practices of those who have read the Bible in the last year, 78% read it monthly, 54% weekly and 17% daily (Goff et al., 2017, pp. 6–29). As noted already, those percentages are highest among older readers, less-educated readers, Southern readers and, especially, among people of colour. But even among those who have not read the Bible in the last year, 50% believe the Bible to be the inspired word of God (Goff et al., 2017, pp. 7–9 and compare Ford et al., 2019, pp. 15–17).

When those who said that they did read their Bibles in the IUPUI survey were asked what they read and why, correspondents highlighted the importance of the Psalms and of passages which brought consolation and comfort (Goff et al., 2017, p. 13). Moreover, it was noted that most people who read the Bible did so not to research issues related to the contemporary socio-political culture wars but rather for personal prayer and devotion (72%), to learn about religion (62%), to explore personal relationships (44%), and to learn about health and healing (36%) (Goff et al., 2017, pp. 16–21). These correspondents regard the Bible as a consoling, helpful, therapeutic text – a text which can bring them support and personal benefit in a changing and often pressurized world. Later in this book, I will explore Christian Smith's construct of 'moralistic therapeutic deism' (MTD) as one way in which young people construct a performative theology in the present day (Smith and Denton, 2005). I will return to look at how this works within Day's exploration of performative practice, as well as other Global North analogues of MTD such as the so-called happy midi-narrative (Collins-Mayo and Beaudoin, 2010). In the use of social media, in the data I offer for popular Bible verses and in this exploration of the Bible in contemporary society, there is a clear sense that Bible engagement is often about performance or social engagement rather than for propositional belief.

It is worth looking at two further books in a little more detail to consider this: James Bielo's *Social Life of Scripture* (Bielo, 2009) and Louise Lawrence's *Word in Place* (Lawrence, 2009). Each of the books focus on the performative outcomes of Bible engagement – on how people read the Bible in their own contexts and how those readings are lived out in everyday life. So, in *The Social Life of Scripture*, Bielo (2009) gathers together a collection of essays about social engagement and the Bible from a wealth of different global and ecclesial contexts. The various essays portray both actual engagement with the Bible in specific contexts, but also the sense that the Bible remains an iconic text for many and so its influence often outweighs specific engagement with it. So, in the chapter relating to the contemporary crisis within the Church of England, Rosamond Rodman (in Bielo, 2009, pp. 100–113) notes the cultural differences within this crisis: "Global South allies foreground scripture, not context . . . refer repeatedly to the supreme authority of scriptures . . . identifying with scripture" over against their identity (Rodman in Bielo, 2009, pp. 108–9) with generally more progressive Global North Anglicans, whose focus is much more on the context within which the contemporary Church is working (Rodman in Bielo, 2009, pp. 105–107). So, Rodman's key example is of a Global South bishop using actual scriptural texts against an individual which are rebuffed by that individual through a progressive reading of the Bible in the context of inclusion. In the end, Rodman argues that the specific texts are much less important in the crisis than "the agency of scripture – the power that certain parties attribute to it and the things it is made to do" (Rodman in Bielo, 2009, p. 111).

Similarly, Malley's contribution to the collection, "Understanding the Bible's Influence" offers an anthropological exploration of "Biblicism: the complex of ideas and practices that surround the Bible", practices which include long-term epistemological processes of associating doctrines with the Bible or momentary, quotidian practices of retrieving Bible verses from digital devices. Biblicism, Malley argues (in Bielo, 2009, pp. 194–195) is about how people actually use and experience the Bible. Indeed, Malley refers back to the contributions to the volume as a whole as relating "scripture use to broader social processes of legitimization, discourse formation, and identity formation" (Malley in Bielo, 2009, p. 196). As such, Malley explores the interaction between the concepts of 'the Bible' and 'God's word' as authoritative discourse within society in general and in the Church. Within the collection of essays in the volume, Malley argues, there is plenty of evidence that 'God's word' exceeds the concept of 'the Bible', indeed that 'the Bible' is a derivation of the concept of 'God's word'. As such, the Bible's authority is derived from its links to socially accepted authoritative discourse "rather than in any doctrine of divine inspiration" (Malley in Bielo, 2000, p. 199).[2]

For Malley, the connection between 'God's Word' and 'the Bible' explains some of the fluidity around concepts of 'the Bible' within different ages, cultures and societies. 'The Bible', he argues, acts as a fluid concept allowing different interpretations, different translations, different rememberings of Bible texts – even the kind of iconic or totemic concepts of the Bible within American culture explored by Berlinerblau. What's important within Biblicism is not the text but the concept. Moreover, the fluidity allows practitioners to alter their specific focus on 'what the Bible says' – so increasingly evangelicals, especially in the non-American Global North/minority world, are keen to point to what the Bible says about environmentalism, progressive attitudes to sexuality and same-sex relations, and postcolonialism – issues which can be traced back through history but which also reflect specific issues important with contemporary social contexts (Malley in Bielo, 2009, p. 203). In other words, different people perform their Biblicism in different ways – some through a deep engagement with scripture and through devotional reading; others through a sense of the Bible as part of a larger concept of authoritative discourse which includes other texts or political positions; others still who might reject the actual Bible while holding tightly to a concept of the Bible containing some aspect of 'the word of God'. Different people therefore see their positions as 'Biblical', see their religious and civic performances as 'Biblical' but without actually engaging much with the text itself.

Lawrence's volume, *The Word in Place: Reading the New Testament in Contemporary Contexts* (Lawrence, 2009), represents a larger and somewhat mixed corpus of contextual Bible reading research (see, in its many different forms: Paauw, 2016; Davis and Hayes, 2003; Rogers, 2015; Village, 2007; Perrin, 2016; Ford, 2018). As with Bielo, the focus here is on the process of Bible engagement within specific contexts by real readers: the social practice of Bible reading. This work is more consciously centred on the Contextual Bible Study movement (Lawrence, 2009, pp. 13–44), which focuses on 'community/folk consciousness' of the Bible rather than the critical consciousness of the traditional historical critical methodology. As

The contemporary context of Bible engagement 19

such, the focus is on how the Bible passage is read in and through the lens of the reading group's consciousness and context and how those insights might contribute to ongoing praxis (Lawrence, 2009, pp. 16–20) – a process which Lawrence likens to Chris Rowlands' concept of the actualization of the text in specific contemporary action (Lawrence, 2009, p. 20). But it is clear that this process is also what Lawrence calls 'a hermeneutics of presence': the creation of a space in which ordinary people and their engagement with the Biblical text might happen (Lawrence, 2009, pp. 121–122).

Critically, this research reflects actual Bible readers – folk Bible readers – within their own context. How are ordinary people engaging with the Bible? Similarly, the research in this volume focuses on ordinary online engagement with the Bible on social media, drawing specifically on popular culture and the everyday use of the Bible rather than on specific processes of Bible engagement demanded by the Church or by any other parachurch organization. It will be important to think through both the context of that engagement but also the tendency to produce a performance which reflects a sense of identity (Day, 2010; Malley in Bielo, 2009; Lawrence, 2009).

How will I do this?

Chapter 2 will explore some more background – how the Bible and digital culture has been explored within Digital Religion and how social media helps people to perform within their own constructions of identity, while at the same time conforming or usurping society's assumptions about that identity.

Chapters 3 and 4 will engage with the core section of my research: a detailed look at the most popular Bible verses liked, highlighted or shared across a range of different social media platforms and across a decade. The Bible verses will be collated and analyzed to see if there has been a shift in the kind of verses liked or shared and whether this conforms to other patterns that have been seen in the relevant social contexts.

In Chapter 5, I will look at the interplay between Day's concept of 'performative belief' and another possible construction of faith identity (Smith's construal of MTD), as well as the potential impact of changes in media ecology and mediatization of religion.

In the conclusion, I will explore the findings of the research, explore some possible alternative explanations of the data and conclude the research with some proposals for further study.

Notes

1 The quotation should actually close with "Western man" but has been updated on ground of inclusivity.
2 Of course, there are others, including many theologians, who might disagree!

2 The Bible, social media and digital culture

In *Neuromancer*, William Gibson (1984, p. 67) defined 'cyberspace' as:

> a consensual hallucination experienced daily by billions of legitimate operators, in every nation, by children being taught mathematical concepts. . . . A graphical representation of data abstracted from the banks of every computer in the human system. Unthinkable complexity. Lines of light ranged in the nonspace of the mind, clusters and constellations of data. Like city lights, receding.

Cyberspace, back then, was indeed another place, a place of numbers and data, a creation in the nonspace of the mind. But Gibson also talked about the 'eversion of cyberspace', or of the 'invasion' of cyberspace into the real world:

> Cyberspace, not so long ago, was a specific elsewhere, one we visited periodically, peering into it from the familiar physical world. Now cyberspace has everted. Turned itself inside out. Colonized the physical. Making Google a central and evolving structural unit not only of the architecture of cyberspace, but of the world.
>
> (Gibson, 2010, n.p.)

Where once the internet was 'somewhere' we went – another place, in a different realm, a 'second life' – ever more immersive technology has changed our experience of the internet. As Christine Hine argues (2015) the internet is now embedded, embodied and everyday. We no longer 'go to' the internet, because it is actually everywhere around us both in mundane objects (through the increasing reach of the internet of things) as well as in sophisticated computing devices masquerading as mobile phones, smart speakers and TVs, watches and, increasingly, medical (surveillance) tech. The everyday, immersive, social aspect of digital culture transforms the very technology itself. So, the mobile phone originally provided the user with an ability to make and receive calls away from a fixed line. However, recent reports from industry experts and the press point out that most smartphones are now used much more for watching videos, texting, internet searching/browsing and gaming, than for making voice calls (Mirani, 2014; OfCom, 2018).

This eversion of cyberspace is not just about the physical omnipresence of the internet in digital culture but also about its powerful hermeneutical presence as explored in Laurence Scott's provocative Four Dimensional Human (2016). Whilst the early internet may have acted as though 'what happens in cyberspace remains on cyberspace', nowadays we all know the naivety of that point of view. Indeed, the physical eversion of cyberspace in the everyday, and its subsequent pervasion into the mundane, means that it actively shapes so much of the culture in which we live. So, whether we think of the preference for texting among teenagers, or the development of different so-called tribes of Digital Millennials, or the impact of fake news on politics and contemporary social action, cyberspace is not something 'out there', "a consensual hallucination" (Gibson, 1984, p. 67), but rather a real-world experience increasingly imposed upon us and potentially impacting the whole of our lives in every sphere from relationships (Baym, 2010) to social communication (Zsupan-Jerome, 2014; Turkle, 2016) and ethics (Balkan, 2018), both in books (Sargeant & Tagg, 2014) and on screens (Kalogridis, 2018 and Coogler, 2018).

This book is founded on the eversion of cyberspace as a hermeneutical phenomenon. My basic hypothesis is that I can trace a shift from propositional texts to therapeutic texts in both the 'liking' and 'sharing' of Bible texts in contemporary social media. The result is a shift in public engagement with the Bible and the public display of the Bible through those texts. In other words, whereas once John 3:16 was the 'poster boy' text of the 20th century, the latest star is Jeremiah 29:11. John 3:16 is propositional: it talks of a God who, motivated through love, intervenes in the world through his son, Jesus, to bring salvation to those who believe in him. God acts; God intervenes; humanity is the object of that intervention. In Jeremiah 29:11, God (although the text only says "I") states that he knows the plans he has to bring blessing and prosperity to his people, to offer them "hope and a future." In an increasingly dystopian world, such a promise is indeed attractive. However, it is a promise of something yet to come (and in Jeremiah 29:10, we are warned that this will be a 70-year wait) and an intervention which is pushed into the future. It's a much more distant picture of divine intervention: a therapeutic bon mot rather than a declaration of intent to intervene in humanity's affairs in the here and now.

To date there have been several studies exploring the Bible in digital culture (Dyer, 2011; Cheong, 2012, 2014; Byers, 2014; Hutchings, 2014; Siker, 2017; Weaver, 2017a, 2017b; Phillips, 2018). In the most in-depth of these to date, Jeffrey Siker (2017) explores the history of computing and the Bible, the context of Bible engagement in the contemporary USA and some of the issues around Bible reading in digital culture. Siker argues from the start that the Digital Bible is "but one component of an increasingly digital church" (Siker, 2017, p. 2). The scope of the book is much larger than the contemporary digital experience. Siker also explores issues concerning both the development of Biblical technology from scrolls to codex to printing (pp. 13–34), as well as the development of academic research incorporating digital methods and the subsequent development of Digital Bibles (pp. 35–56) and the issues related to reading texts under glass (pp. 57–96). In later chapters, he looks at some preliminary exploration of survey data on reading Digital Bibles (pp. 97–124). Probably the most significant chapter explores the hermeneutical effect of digital transformation: the potential for the text to be left without boundaries, a free-floating text which can be manipulated within digital culture (pp. 124–182). In Chapter 7 (pp. 183–208), he explores Bible engagement on four social media platforms: Twitter, Facebook, YouTube and in blogging. I will look at this chapter in a moment, before taking a look at the Bible and computer programs, and making some concluding remarks on potential problems with the Bible in digital format.

In his chapter on the Bible and social media (pp. 183–208), Siker argues that there is the potential for the Bible to be transmuted from a text into image and sound – for the text to become multimedia. I have already noted that the Bible has always been a (multi-)mediated text (Poleg, 2013; Edwards, 2015), part and parcel of both the textual, material and conceptual world, as much at home in the arts, architecture and the everyday as in the Church. Siker's point, though, is that digital culture continues the transformation of the Bible, critical to the Reformation period, into the vernacular (p. 185): "the de-sacralization of the Bible on digital devices of all kinds" offers "a new vernacular of Christian faith for reading, hearing and watching the Bible". In other words, if we want to explore how citizens of the digital age are engaging with the Bible, then it is to these new platforms that we should look.

Siker is clear that with this new vernacular comes some interesting side effects – from Twitter mega-pastors to celebrity YouTube channels, both of which seek to present a particular form of Christianity but also to dominate the dialogue around the Bible. So, Stephen Smith of *OpenBible* estimated that in 2015, 50% of the "40 million [Bible] verses shared on Twitter . . . came from Bible spam accounts – accounts which do nothing but tweet Bible verses all day". (Smith, 2015). This suggests that Pauline Hope Cheong's concept of the flow of spiritual tweets is heavily polluted with automated messaging from powerful Christian lobbies. Of course, this is all part of the larger issues about authority structures around the Bible which Cheong (2016) explores in her work on social media, pastors and

The Bible, social media and digital culture 23

digital engagement. In his subsequent study of four areas of social media engagement with the Bible, Siker points to blogging/vlogging as the most open channel for serious reflection on the text. Since the other two chosen channels are microblogging sites, this seems to be obvious. But Siker does raise the point that aspects of microblogging have always been part of the Church's Biblical discourse: references to Bible texts, allusions, quotations, pepper Christian discourse from the very start (Siker, 2017, p. 194), whilst also arguing that such microblogging of texts tends to leave out the literary context within which those texts have meaning. In other words, whereas blogging/vlogging provide opportunity for a more rounded and contextual interpretation of scripture, microblogging offers a much 'thinner' experience of the text – either a brief quotation, a paraphrase or a reference, something Siker calls "a minimalist text" (p. 197). This issue with the 'thinness' of microblogging develops into a critique of the superficiality of digital culture, reflecting some of the criticisms of the internet discussed in Nicholas Carr's *The Shallows* (Carr, 2011). Siker proposes that microblogging has a tendency to make the Biblical text superficial, to create "disembodied maxims, not unlike what you find in a fortune cookie", while at the same time acknowledging that a tweet can act as a summary of a much larger portion of scripture (Siker, 2017, p. 206).

Siker's study is an invaluable contribution to our understanding of the Bible in digital culture. His understanding that digital Bible engagement on social media extends Bible engagement into the vernacular of the present age is profound. But if that is the case then it is important to actually hear what people are saying rather than to seek to constrain that conversation into the language of the Church. In other words, what verses of the Bible are being used online, what passages shared, what concepts used? If we can read social media engagement, then we may get a better and more profound understanding of Bible engagement in contemporary culture. Moreover, again going back to Abby Day (2010), we will find a performance of belief rather than an assertion of faith expected by authority structures and institutions. Social media has the potential to reveal something important about how the Bible is perceived within digital culture.

In a number of articles exploring the use of Twitter in religious community practice, Pauline Hope Cheong picks up similar themes to Siker but analyzes the issues quite differently (Cheong, 2012, 2014, 2016). Cheong defines microblogging as "an increasingly popular phenomenon whereby users engage in composing brief multimedia updates and sending them via web-based applications such as text messaging, instant messaging, email or on the web" (Cheong, 2012, p. 191). She proposes that because of the affordances of Twitter's platform, "one likely future vision for Twitter is to be a micro-sharing and mobilization platform for religious communities" and that such use could "perhaps even alter and broaden the notion of religious social capital building" (Cheong, 2012, p. 192). In another article, Cheong picks up Claire Diaz-Ortiz's comment in the *New York Times:* "Pastors tell me, Twitter is just made for the Bible" (2014, p. 2). This article explores the development, use and interpretation of Bible tweets, "micro sacred texts", "spiritual tweets", questioning whether microblogging facilitates "new (re) presentations of Scripture in brief forms" (Cheong, 2014, p. 3), which in turn lead to new practices of interpretation and authority. Cheong's default position is not to critique microblogging but rather to assess such practice as religious performance in itself – a kind of digital ethnography. Spurred on by Diaz-Ortiz's enthusiasm, she posits the development of microblogging itself into a kind of spiritual exercise, a form of prayer. But Cheong (2016) also explores the creation of an online persona for both pastors and their churches to both establish and extend the authority structure amongst the believing community. This shift from the democratization of everyone tweeting spiritual tweets, to pastors establishing authority and correct practice is a sign of the Church conforming to celebrity culture, argues Cheong (2016).

Certainly, there have been conscious attempts to develop this into formal acts of worship, such as @poppytweets in the UK several years ago, or through the Facebook account of D-Church or through @sanctuaryfirst's online engagement. So, in her exploration of worship practices in digital culture, Teresa Berger (2017, p. 3) gives a list of the kind of spiritual expressions available online:

> It is clear that both very old and entirely new liturgical practices are flourishing online. They range from broadcasts of liturgical celebrations over the internet, virtual altars, online chapels, cyber rosaries, prayer apps with streaming video and image galleries, memorial sites, online pilgrimages, digitally mediated Eucharistic Adoration and novenas to new resources such as a "twomplet" (Compline on Twitter, in tweets), digital Advent and Lenten calendars, and an app for Catholic Meditations on Purgatory. There are also communities of faith that exist online alone, for example in web-based interactive virtual reality environments such as Second Life. Clearly, digitally mediated liturgical life is rich, multifaceted, and effervescent. It is also ceaselessly expanding.

Self-(re)presentation and community development on social media platforms such as Twitter and Facebook have become closely related aspects of research. Since so many people spend so much time engaged with such platforms and because those platforms are built on the key concept of social connectivity, it is obvious that these platforms are a good place to explore contemporary spirituality and practices. So, in a section exploring the 'digital turn', Berger (2017, p. 6) urges ritual and liturgical scholars to look online for new spiritual practices and the embedding of old practice in new forms and provides an excellent list of places to start in her footnotes. Indeed, some of that work is found in the wealth of literature around Digital Religion.

Digital Religion is an ever-increasing field of study – exploring both offline religion's use of digital means for communication and advertising as well as online expression of religious practice, and thus exploring Chris Helland's differentiation between religion online and online religion (Helland, 2001, 2005, 2012). The wider field of Digital Religion is mapped in several monographs and edited collections (Campbell, 2005, 2010, 2013; Campbell and Garner, 2016; Cheong, 2012, 2014; Cheruvallil-Contractor and Shakkour, 2015) and in the website of the Network for New Media, Religion and Digital Culture Studies (NNMRDC, 2019) dedicated to Digital Religion, which provides an excellent blog and an updated bibliography citing almost 700 works. In their contribution to *Digital Methodologies in the Sociology of Religion* (Cheruvallil-Contractor and Shakkour, 2015, pp. 1–12), Heidi Campbell and Brian Altenhofen (2015) identify four different waves within Digital Religion studies: descriptive, categorical, theoretical and convergent. The 'waves' can be compared to similar developmental patterns within the Digital Humanities more broadly, such as those explored by David Berry in his major edited collection on this area of contemporary research (Berry, 2012, pp. 1–20). I have worked recently with other scholars associated with the CODEC Research Centre to map Digital Theology's place within Digital Religion and the wider field of Digital Humanities (Phillips, Schiefelbein and Kurlberg, 2019). Specifically theological reflections on digital culture are both numerous and of mixed quality and often aimed at the popular market. Some of the most outstanding not mentioned already include Jana Bennet's work, Aquinas on the Web (2015), John Dyer's work, *From the Garden to the City*, (2011), Deanna Thompson's work, *The Virtual Body of Christ in a Suffering World* (2016), and finally Daniella Zsupan-Jerome's *Connected Toward Communion: The Church and Social Communication in the Digital Age* (2014).

I have already noted the work of Cheong which explores microblogging as a spiritual act and as part of the identity formation of both pastors and their churches. But tweeting is part of the identity formation of everyone who tweets – it establishes a persona: "defining the person directly, providing a vocabulary of motives, explicating moral values, and articulating group categorization and affiliation" (Cheong, 2016, citing Alvesson and Willmott, 2002). Social media acts a focus for community development – for creating communities, for communicating across communities and also for expressing individual identity within/across those communities.

A good deal of research has been done about the way that the expression of identity and community works on Twitter, of the reality of what Richard Rogers calls "network sociality" (2014, p. xiv) in the much larger collection of academic essays exploring Twitter's social engagement and social impact, Twitter and Society (Weller & others, 2014). As Dhiraj Murthy puts it: "Twitter affords a unique opportunity to re-evaluate how communication and culture can be individualistic and communal simultaneously" (2013, p. xi). While there are still public aspects of other social media platforms, Twitter offers theoretical access to any tweeter in the world as long as you know their account identifier (@ name). The platform offers a space for public broadcasting of any message, including religious messages, and access to such a large market for advertising and display has meant that Twitter has developed over the years as a popular broadcast medium for businesses, celebrities and presidents: "Perhaps rather than social circles, Twitter users have audiences" (Rogers, 2014, p. xv; Marwick and boyd, 2011). With an audience ready to consume, often uncritically, and especially if outrage is involved, Twitter has become one of the primary battlefields of our contemporary culture wars (Castells, 2012; Crockett, 2017; Stetzer, 2018). We are, as Chris Rojek puts it so sharply, "constant, often furtive, watchers of the lives of others". But Rojek goes on to point out that those "others" are normally "evanescent wraiths" in a world of "statistical men and women", rather than people we really know (Rojek, 2016, pp. 2–9).

Interaction on Twitter certainly includes religious interaction: celebrities make use of faith allegiance to gain followers and support; religious leaders and preachers of different faiths coach their followers and make the most of political affiliation or religious authority to develop their own quasi-celebrity status online (Marwick and boyd, 2011; Cheong, 2016). Twitter is also a space for the general public to express their own feelings, concerns, love and hates, including their own religious practices and preferences to everyone else on the network. Because Twitter enables any user to address the Twitter public and to send tweets to any other user using their account identifier (@ name), Twitter theoretically offers a flat hierarchy where anyone (celebrity, politician, preacher, 'ordinary citizen' or refugee, of whatever gender identity, whatever age, whatever economic position) can share their thoughts on life. But in reality social networks are relatively limited, because of the various filters applied by both the user and the platform itself. As Dimitar Nikolev and others point out (Nikolev, 2015), Facebook applies three filters: the social network, the feed population algorithm and the user's own content selection. This kind of process limits what you see on Twitter, necessarily. With millions of users and 500 million tweets sent every day, it would be impossible to follow the full flow of Twitter. So, each user normally follows a limited number of people (social network filter) and will normally read their tweets, either through their own feed (feed population filter), or through lists or notifications (user filter). Users therefore create their own filter bubbles, often engaging only with those who are like-minded, a process called 'homophily': the tendency for people to prefer connecting with others with similar worldviews than with others with diametrically opposed views (Nikolov et al., 2015), or, as Day puts it, "the comforting sense of cultural homogeneity" (Day, 2011, p. 49). The filter bubble affect limits 'network sociality' as well as potentially facilitating confirmation bias and certainly creating a fertile ground for polarization and misinformation (Conover et al., 2011). To some extent then, calling social media a form of 'network sociality' should not be the same as thinking everyone is on social media, nor that everyone's views are shared or heard equally on social media.

Twitter plays well to the human need for self-display and, as such, the constant stream of social media banality and the propensity to self-advertisement may point to implicit processes of user identity maintenance and development as much as to the background machinations of market capitalism/corporatism (Rogers, 2014). Again, Rojek (2016, pp. 8–9), points to the ambiguity in current attitudes towards data privacy: on the one hand, terrorism is used by the corporate state to deprive us of privacy and to ratchet up state surveillance and instill a sense of paranoia about data piracy and hacking, but on the other hand, countless people are sharing intimate details about their lives, loves and social practices openly on public social media sites. Clearly, the need or desire to share, the potential of developing social connection, outweighs the need for privacy.

The desire to share and the sheer banality which characterizes social media (pictures of meals, cats, daily routines, holidays, reactions to media culture) represent together an interesting topic of research. The kind of banality on social media consists of what linguists sometimes refer to as 'phatic communication' (Rogers, 2014, p. xiv; Varis and Blommaert, 2017; compare Hjarvard, 2011, p. 128): the background noise to our lives, the social radio playing in the corner, the sense that others are present with us, the sense of conviviality.

> The continuous flow of the day, the week and the time of the year once acquired its structure through the daily chiming of the church bells, prayers at specific times and particular seasonal religious feasts. Today, daily life has become structured, not least, through habits of media consumption, television time schedules and serial formats.
> (Hjarvard, 2011, p. 209, compare de Certeau, 1984)

As such, social media provides the social context for contemporary life and provides what Gunter Senft (cited in Varis and Blommaert, 2017, p. 2) calls "utterances that are said to have exclusively social, bonding functions . . . for keeping the channels open". Phatic communication in turn leads to a sense of conviviality and connection to the general flow of daily life. Social media populates our social space with ideas, suggestions and emotions – indeed, it populates social space in general. But social media also helps us to fill that space with those emotions and ideas with which we agree and with which we think others will also empathize.

Murthy (2013, pp. 27–50) notes that in doing this, in creating potentially empathetic social spaces, we also provide a sense of telepresence or social presence for those who 'listen in', for those who read our tweets or view our Facebook posts. In this space, we feel connected to others (even celebrities) through their own (carefully constructed) use of banality ("I can see what this celebrity ate for their dinner", "I can see this star doing their makeup"). Citing Christian Licoppe, Murthy argues:

> [P]hysically absent parties "[gain] presence through the multiplication of mediated communication gestures on both sides." In other words, a constancy of presence is felt through multiplied interactions – a process Twitter is inherently designed for.
>
> (Murthy, 2013, p. 39)

Moreover, in this place of 'absent-present' social presence (Baym, 2010), we are encouraged to develop our own personas, our own re-presentations of who we are. So, Nancy Baym and danah boyd point out that users, encouraged by telepresence and conviviality, "actively apply the affordances of new technologies to advance their own creative and instrumental objectives" (Baym and boyd, 2012; compare Cheong, 2012, 2014, 2016). In other words, social media provides the user with a theoretically safe space both for self-presentation and, by provoking more and more communication from the user (Heidegger's concept [1977, p. 14] of 'drawing out', 'calling forth' more, *Herausfordern*), prompts the user to articulate something (more) of their own identity, to cultivate aspects of their own communication and social presence. Indeed, Rojek (2016, pp. 6–8) makes use of Stanley Milgram's concept of the familiar stranger, the people who populate the same social spaces that we do but with whom we have an implicit agreement not to actually communicate. Rojek argues that we break this implicit agreement on social media by reaching out to the familiar stranger (acquaintances who are now 'friends' on social media) through lurking, liking, replying to comments, adapting our social interactions and broadening the sense of community around us. The affordances of social media, the buzz we get from replies and encounters, push us towards much weaker social boundaries and different sorts of social interactions.

Such self-representation on social media, often based on Erving Goffman's interactional theory, is the subject of a growing body of research (Goffman, 1959, 1963; Hogan, 2010; Marwick and boyd, 2010; Marwick and boyd, 2011; Baym and boyd, 2012). How much do people reveal about their inner life and how much of online representation is itself an artificial retelling of their reality, either in hope or despair? Do people reveal their true self, or what we might call a 'photoshopped self', a self for social media, which matches the affordances and preferences of the particular social media platform itself? Indeed, how much do people assume/wish that their 'photoshopped self', their social media construction of their self is, in fact, their true identity – something which might be called 'selfie dysmorphia', as explored in a recent article by Elle Hunt, who investigated the growing phenomenon of people taking filtered selfies to plastic surgeons and asking for treatment to make them look like their image (Hunt, 2019).

This book explores the concepts around creation/extension of community and identity through the use of social media and the subsequent morphing or recasting of both through the habitual use of/self-performance within social media.

I want to ask questions about the kind of Bible verses which are habitually liked or shared on social media (and so 'popular'). How do people who signify their liking for Bible verses, or seek to identify with a specific verse through retweeting it or sharing it, understand this to feed into their social media persona? Does this practice help to increase their social capital in some specific circle of friends either by the tweets themselves ("Look, I'm Biblical like you!") or by showing that they are the kind of people who tweet Bible tweets ("Look, I think this social performance is important", "Look, I'm an evangelical"). Of course, few of us do any of this consciously, but our use of social media in public (virtual) space does impact how others/our audience view us – and also affects the algorithms which push social media in our direction for now they know that we like seeing tweets with the Bible in them.

Social engagement, of course, changes over time. We tweak our own social media performance, our list of friends and acquaintances, and we also tweak what we share online. Goffman argued that individuals give an 'idealized' rather than authentic version of themselves, tweaking their behaviour dependent on their current audience in a process which he termed "impression management" (Goffman, 1959, p. 22; Hogan, 2010, p. 378). Interactional theory depends upon the co-presence (in Goffman 'real' presence, of course) of the audience and the subject's ongoing reaction to that audience. Goffman argues indeed that while the subject presents 'front stage' their idealized persona (we might say 'their photoshopped self'), at the same time 'backstage' is "a place . . . where the impression fostered by the performance is knowingly contradicted as a matter of course" (Goffman, 1959, p. 112; Hogan, 2010, p. 378). For Goffman, at least, co-present performance is essential: interaction depends on synchronous, visual engagement between the actor and a specific audience and assumptions that for this performance this persona counts, however many underlying issues the backstage leakage raises for us. The question is whether the kind of absent-present relationship of asynchronous social media engagement has the same effect on the performer's impression management. It seems likely that an audience's absent-presence does indeed have a similar effect on the performer (Marwick and boyd, 2010; Baym and boyd, 2012)

It is worth noting that in her adaptation of interaction theory to electronic culture, Karin Knorr Cetina (2009) rejects much of this setting, holding only to the concept of the importance of interaction within a specific context, and so creates the arena of the 'synthetic situation', a concept which Murthy advocates (Murthy, 2013, pp. 42–44). Social media engagement, Murthy argues, offers something akin to Cetina's 'synthetic situation' – a mediated interaction on screens. So, Bernie Hogan argues for a distinction between 'performance' spaces based on interaction between co-present actors engaged in synchronous and responsive interaction and 'exhibition' spaces based on asynchronous interaction and the display of (digital) artefacts – the 'exhibition space' would be a 'synthetic situation' (Hogan, 2010, p. 377). In contrast, Marwick and boyd (2010) compare the relatively fixed and self-aware presentation of the self on personal homepages ('exhibition' space?) to the much more fluid presentation of the self (akin to 'personal branding') within social media.

Whilst social media demands variety in self-presentation dependent on the audience, the reception of social media and the plurality of potential audiences "ruptures the ability to vary self-presentation . . . and manage discrete impressions" (Marwick and boyd, 2010, pp. 115–117). Social media ruptures the 'performance space' and the ability of the social media actor to create discrete self-presentations as Goffman proposed – there are too many individuals with whom to engage and they are all absent-present. Indeed, the way Twitter works, "it is virtually impossible for Twitter users to account for their potential audience, let alone actual readers" (Marwick and boyd, 2010, p. 117). As such, while normal social media users present a self-presentation based on concepts of authenticity, celebrities tend to follow fewer people and are able to present the synthetic persona which is the basis for their own celebrity status. This kind of performance collapses only when backstage leakage overwhelms it and the press notice!

For most social media users, anxiety about potential audience(s) and the presentation of the persona itself remains a reality. Many choose to adopt the practices of celebrity personas – we become micro-celebrities performing to the world (Marwick and boyd, 2011). Such anxiety might be compared to Goffman's 'backstage anxiety' – but as Hogan points out, the audience are always aware of the backstage anyway, and so it is not the same as a kind of private reflection on personal branding of someone still to perform: backstage is backstage, not the green room (Hogan, 210, p. 380). As such, advice is given to Twitter users to reflect long and hard before tweeting in order to create the most favourable presentation of the self. But how do you create a personal brand on a platform which actively creates 'context collapse' – where work colleagues, friends, political allies and opponents, influencers, celebrities and corporate customer service accounts are all potential readers; where the potential actor (still in the green room) has no idea who the audience might be or if indeed there will be any audience at all? (Marwick and boyd, 2010, p. 122)

As I mentioned earlier, the mismatch between Goffman's interactionism and online media leads Hogan to argue that social media is an 'exhibition space', distinguishing "between performance as an ephemeral act and performance as a recorded act" and referencing Walter Benjamin's argument that reproduction lacks "the unique 'aura' of the original object" (Hogan, 2010, p. 380). Indeed, as Benjamin later argues, in film the actor does not interact with the audience and the audience does not engage with the actor, rather both engage with the camera (Benjamin, 1967, p. 268). When the audience becomes invisible, as Benjamin's prescient words make clear, the medium itself becomes both the lens through which actors present themselves and the lens through which the audience observes the performance – the medium has become the message. As noted earlier, Baym and boyd (2012, p. 323) discuss the potential plurality and diversity of social media audiences in terms of context collapse, querying the very concept of a stable or visible audience with whom the social media actor might engaged. They too argue that mass communication cuts off the actor from the audience, but suggest that social media seeks to re-engage actor and audience, but never to the same extent as in a co-present performance since the actor cannot engage face to face with such a disparate and asynchronous audience. To some extent this is similar to Rojek's suggestion that social media breaks the implicit non-communication agreement between known/familiar strangers in our public social space. Social media encourages us to connect with people we don't know to create a new relational hub in society thus offering new patterns of interaction, connectivity and conviviality (Rojek, 2016, pp. 8–9).

Hogan's definition of exhibition space is worth quoting in full:

> An exhibition site can now be defined as a site (typically online) where people submit reproducible artifacts (read: data). These artifacts are held in storehouses (databases). Curators (algorithms designed by site maintainers) selectively bring artifacts out of storage for particular audiences. The audience in these spaces consists of those who have and those who make use of access to the artifacts. This includes those who respond, those who lurk, and those who acknowledge or are likely to acknowledge.
>
> (Hogan, 2010, p. 381)

I think this is a retelling of something like the Facebook environment. Twitter, like many more recent forms of social media engagement, does not quite follow the same rules. However, the kind of social engagement within Hogan's 'exhibition space' does resemble the social interaction within social media in general more closely than Goffman's concept of a 'live' performance space with a co-present audience with whom the actor interacts. In fact, there are Goffman-like performance spaces online – perhaps in Facebook Live/vlogging/Twitch and multi-player online gaming in particular. Indeed, some aspects of social media such as Facebook comments, Messenger/Whatsapp conversations and Twitter mentions/direct messaging may well fit better within interactionism: actors present themselves in a specific way to a specific co-present audience. In contrast, Twitter curates the tweets of those followed by a user into their feed, offers new suggestions for others to follow and sends notifications about tweets the user might have missed, along with the ever-present ads. Meanwhile, the public audience and the following audience engage with the user's own generated tweets through the Twitter interface either on a computer or mobile device. The interaction is with the platform presenting the user's tweets (archived data) rather than directly with the user – this seems to be a kind of 'exhibition space'.

In her exploration of the 'twitter of faith', Cheong (2012) proposed that Twitter creates various forms of 'microblogging rituals' well suited to build and maintain religious communities – a way of creating affiliation and conviviality and so a sense of social presence: an 'exhibition space' across an online community: "a stream of lived sacred experiences, thereby ideologically connecting Twitter believers in real time" (Cheong, 2012, p. 193). Cheong's research has focused on the development of community and authority within specific church communities and has a much stronger understanding of the role of Twitter to address specific audiences. She would regard Twitter as a place of live religious performance rather than as a place to view curated artefacts: the world of religious leaders cultivating followers. But the accrual of social capital and persuasive communication within these 'exhibition spaces' is precisely the development of authority and power which Cheong refers to. Religious leaders no longer need to rely on an ephemeral public performance – that performance can now be repeatedly delivered in smaller, more manageable chunks and distributed to the waiting masses. The media itself reinforces the public performance and creates even great authority for the leader as well as social cohesion through the network as followers like and reshare those nuggets of data.

From a different perspective, John B. Weaver (2017b, p. 152) rejects such usage as inappropriate and calls into question the automation of Bible-verse or Bible-teacher-quote sharing online:

[T]he spamming of social media users by automated, computer-generated messages containing Bible verses is generating a digital environment in which verses are falsely represented as "sent" by individuals and also divorced from attention to Biblical and social contexts. . . . Th[e] growing automation of scripture citations in the social media sphere is a combination of misinformation and information overload, both of which desensitize viewers to the power of scriptures because of their mass quantity and questionable quality.

(Weaver, 2017b, p. 152)

Both arguments point to the important role which 'sacred tweets' play in the ongoing development of Christian practice within social media. Whether those tweets represent a data repository of artefacts accessed asynchronously or a live stream of sacred experiences, Cheong and Weaver argue that such tweets are deployed by authority figures/church leaders as a database/reference book or what we might once have called a 'rule' or 'canon' for believers, through which they seek to impose authoritative common belief among communities of faith (Cheong, 2012; Campbell and Garner, 2016).

Of course, the sheer abundance of global social media engagement easily overwhelms the tweeting of even the most prolific religious leader. In this way, the tweeting of individuals creates an 'ordinary canon' of expressions about the Bible – a trend which might reveal what ordinary believers think about the Bible and seek to project into the online world (Astley and Francis, 2013). It is the impact of this ordinary Bible tweeting which this research will examine rather than the tweeting of religious leaders or famous preachers – a subject which other scholars have explored already (Cheong, 2013, 2014; Condone, 2014; Weaver, 2017b).

Tweeting the Bible, and in a different way retweeting the Bible, indeed engaging with the Bible on social media by liking, sharing or bookmarking is itself a form of self-representation. It explicitly associates the social media user with a powerful religio-social icon, 'the Bible'. Moreover, since it is often specific verses which are shared/liked/bookmarked, it suggests a greater familiarity than simply knowing what 'the Bible' is. Tweeting/sharing specific verses of the Bible could suggest an intimacy between the social media user and the actual text rather than 'the Bible' as a concept. On one hand, this could be the self-presentation of a Bible-centric Christian or it could be someone trying to be seen as such or trying to engage with a community of such people. On the other hand, it could be someone retweeting or liking a Bible verse tweeted by someone else and so co-opting the original message for their purposes or for creating a sense of affiliation between the user and a specific culture. So, Murthy explores Goffman's theory of re-embedding texts as a core aspect of Twitter's retweet feature which "generates wholly new audiences which feel the utterance to be originating from the retweeter . . . [even when] the retweet most often bears reference to the original Twitterer" (Murthy, 2013, p. 45). Similarly, celebrity followers often retweet celebrity tweets in order to gain a sense of affiliation/conviviality with the celebrity social media user (Murthy, 2013, p. 45. See also Marwick and boyd, 2010, p. 115; Marwick and boyd, 2011, p. 147).

Conclusion

We have seen that social media engagement with the Bible needs to be explored within the context of social media engagement and the presentation of self. This is a complex field and brings in exploration of personal relationship within the digital age, especially the concept of absent-presence (Baym, 2010). Users engage in social media to develop relationships and to present something about themselves to the audience they themselves curate. As such, social media engagement with the Bible is itself part of the so-called photoshopped self – a form of 'front staging' a person's Bible engagement. To some extent this is a highly personal endeavour, an endeavour in which we have seen at least one group of digitally engaged Bible-centric individuals choose not to engage. However, I am concerned not with individual performances but rather the impact on the public expression of the Bible on social media which all these performances together create.

This research is primarily concerned with how 'ordinary' social media users engage with the Bible within digital culture. They do this both through passive forms of engagement such as searching for Bible verses and reading/listening (consuming?) sections of the Bible both on apps and websites as well as through active forms of engagement – especially through liking, sharing or bookmarking Bible verses. Passive forms, searching or consuming of the Bible can only really be seen through the build up of data, but active forms create historical records within social media itself as people actively perform their social media engagement on the channels by liking, highlighting, bookmarking and sharing verses. This Bible engagement, both passive and active, has been collated into lists of popular Bible verses mostly by *YouVersion* and *BibleGateway*, the two largest digital platforms for Bible engagement. I use these lists as my major data sources – a kind of 'canon' of ordinary Bible engagement – rather than looking specifically at any exemplar accounts.

In the next chapters, I'll look more closely at those lists – but before this I will develop my own list of Bible verses popular within print culture as a kind of control/comparison to the social media–based lists.

3 Popular Bible verses on social media

I am researching the ordinary social performance of Bible engagement in digital culture, primarily through a series of 20 lists of Bible verses popular on Bible engagement platforms between 2012 and 2019. In this chapter, I will present those lists.

It is perhaps necessary to make clear what I am trying to do with the lists and also to give the reader some choice in how they engage with this research. I have already made clear that I think that Abby Day's exploration of performative belief is important to my analysis of ordinary social performance of Bible engagement in digital culture (Day, 2011). I am aware that this conviction is part and parcel of the hypothesis of this research. I think that social performance mirrors other aspects of performative belief. Mia Lövheim focuses on the importance of performance of belief on social media (Lövheim in Cotter, 2016, pp. 106–8) and James Beckford proposes that more attention needs to be given to the semantic 'moves' that speakers routinely make in order to 'bring off' a performance of belief (Beckford in Cotter, 2016, pp. 102–3). Day herself talks of a belief in practice that is "propositional, affective, embodied and performed" (Day, 2011, p. 6). As such, I think that Day's analysis also links with other trends on the sociology of religion, with Christian Smith's understanding of 'moralistic therapeutic deism' (MTD) (Smith and Denton, 2005), and also with the affordances of contemporary media ecology and the mediatization of religion (Hjarvard, 2011, 2013).

This hypothesis is written up in more depth in Chapter 5 of this book; some readers may wish to read that chapter before the next two chapters. Indeed, how this book was structured has changed repeatedly along with an internal struggle as to whether Chapter 5 should precede this chapter. In the end, the performance will be presented here, and the core concepts that I think lie behind this performance will be explored in Chapter 5.

But having put the major presentation of performative belief and MTD into Chapter 5, it is perhaps worth clarifying again what is meant by 'propositional' and 'therapeutic' verses in what follows. The terms come both from Smith's exploration of MTD (Smith and Denton, 2005) and from Day's exploration of differences between 'propositional' responses to surveys and the actual performance of beliefs within a practice-based faith (Day, 2010, 2011). Importantly, Day prefers to use the two categories of 'anthropocentric' and 'theocentric' (Day, 2011, pp. 156–158). 'Anthropocentric' refers to those conversations Day had with (most) people in which belief centred on human relationships, human agency and perhaps on the role of the dead. In these conversations, God was not mentioned. Here I look at this category through the concept of 'therapeutic', but the issue is the same: the shifting of agency away from God to the human subject, "from the transcendent to the mundane" (Day, 2011, p. 6). Others, a smaller group, have a tendency to talk about salient relationship with God, with God as an active agent in their lives; Day refers to these as 'theocentric' and I use 'propositional', a word which Day also makes use of: "This may reflect a shift from propositional, content-oriented form of belief to a form that is multidimensional and expresses faith and trust" (Day, 2011, p. 158, see also pp. 17–18). This kind of difference has been raised within other scholars' work, notably the shift in Grace Davie's work to 'believing without belonging' or the discussion about the 'spiritual turn' in relation to Linda Woodhead/Stephen Heelas's Kendal Project (Davie, 1994; Heelas and Woodhead, 2005).

So, how might I go about researching the ordinary social performance of Bible engagement in digital culture? Primarily this is achieved through the analysis of publicly available lists of popular Bible verses within the public domain. But I also need to develop a control set of popular Bible verses prior to social media. So, this chapter establishes two samples – an historical sample and a contemporary sample – both longitudinal, both recording Bible engagement and both in English.

> Step 1: create a control sample of longitudinal Bible engagement in books printed in English
> Step 2: create a sample of longitudinal Bible engagement in social media in English

While initial data sources available for both steps provide longitudinal data based on ordinary Bible engagement, there are some important caveats about this research project. We need to remember the larger historical/contextual issues raised in the first two chapters of this book. It is likely that we have never really known how 'ordinary' people have engaged with the Bible. In an earlier chapter, I explored issues about historical Biblical literacy and the concept of the mediated Bible. I have also noted the differences between celebrity engagement and 'ordinary' engagement and noted that the use of 'most popular' lists on social media might help us gain insights into a broader, 'ordinary' level of engagement with the Bible. In addition, to some extent this project looks like it is digital – but it is solidly old-school! I am using published lists of popular verses rather than collating all the data from scratch. I am also limiting myself mostly to texts rather than to images/imagery, YouTube clips or memes. I have chosen to separate out visual culture and textual culture as if that were the perfectly sensible kind of thing to do. But contemporary society, and digital culture specifically, offers a much richer visual diet of Bible engagement, as noted by Katie Edwards and contributors to *Reimagining Biblical Literacy* (Edwards, 2015). But incorporating visual and aural data would have created a massively different project in both scope and site. As such, this is a text-based research project and I will have to leave to others the exploration of Bible shifts through other media.

There are lots of caveats even then, of course. My offline (print) data set will not be the same as the online (social media) data set. The kind of people who historically created printed books (authored, collated, edited, printed) have tended to be from the educated elite in the Global North. As such, I can expect the offline data set to reflect the views of that elite. On the one hand, our use of English as a *lingua franca* may well provide a good comparison with the control set of verses drawn from printed books in English. On the other hand, social media use is much more global in nature, with over half of the world's population now online and with two thirds owning a mobile phone (We Are Social, 2018). As such, the social media data set (the lists of popular Bible verses) is likely to reflect more global engagement with the Bible – and with a global reach also comes a huge amount of actual engagement. Of course, research shows that social media engagement is particularly strong among educated, urban/suburban Digital Millennials (Pew Research, 2018). Indeed, further research has noted that it is particularly this demographic who are tending to engage preferentially with the Bible online, although the article also points out that stated preferences still suggest that all age groups, including Digital Millennials, prefer print to digital versions of the Bible (Weaver, 2017b, p. 150; Ford et al., 2019). Finally, different countries engage with different forms of social media in different ways. As such, platform-specific and country-specific research projects would be needed to get a more localized view of Bible engagement.

Part of the attraction of contemporary social media, of course, is that everyone can have a voice. Indeed, because of the potential of retweeting or sharing posts, people do not need to compose Bible tweets/posts; they can simply share what others have already created. Indeed, many professional Bible tweeters (Bible organizations, online pastors, celebrities) strongly encourage such retweeting (Murthy, 2013, p. 45. See also Marwick and boyd, 2010,

p. 115; Marwick and boyd, 2011, p. 147). Twitter's user base, however, is slanted towards Digital Millennials, especially in the Global North. As such, I will need to take into account current explorations of Digital Millennial faith which might reflect what I see happening in the longitudinal data. I will look at this further in Chapter 4. For the time being, I note that the research does not categorize tweets by age group or geographical location. The lists I have used simply do not provide this type of breakdown of the data, and the organizations concerned seem reluctant to provide the vast swathes of data they own to the academic world.

Step 1: create a control sample of longitudinal Bible engagement in books printed in English

There are two further problems with analyzing lists of popular verses in contemporary social media: firstly, they are so contemporary, so 'of the moment'; and secondly, they are confined to social media. In order to note a shift or a trend, I need to show a long-term pattern or a pattern developing within a different media ecology – in book culture, in visual culture, in homiletics, perhaps? So, if I am going to create a kind of database reflecting popular/ordinary engagement with the Bible in contemporary text-based social media usage, then is it possible to create a database of popular engagement with the Bible in historical offline usage, in printed books for example, to show how those verses were used in a previous media technology? This will at least provide me with some basis for comparing and contrasting Bible engagement within two text-based technologies: print (offline) and social media (online). Moreover, by keeping mostly to the use of the Bible in English and printed books in English, I also provide both an historical comparison to the data in social media and also a medium comparison.

In fact, there is little easily available data about the popularity of different Bible verses across history. Peter Chapman, a freelance digital developer, created a website which lists the top verses referenced across the whole of the internet, using a simple search and display process (Chapman, 2019). In private correspondence (September 8, 2016 and December 17, 2018), Peter described the process in these terms:

> I wrote a PHP script to run Google searches for each verse reference and count the number of results, generating a metric of how referenced every verse was across the internet [after adjusting for false positives]. The results were captured in a MySQL database and I had so much fun looking at particular books or searching for words and ordering the results using this index that I paused the original project and made the indexed verses public instead.

It seems then that the process does collect data from across the whole World Wide Web, which would include historical text archives and perhaps even the Google/COCA text corpora. If so, then this list might reflect some level of historical popularity of Bible verses. Sadly, there are hints that it does not perform quite as well as I hoped; perhaps further work needs to be done on creating an artificial intelligence-based algorithm to create a stronger historical database.

The top ten verses (in their King James translation form) listed on Chapman's website at the end of 2018 remain consistent with those listed in 2016:

1. John 3:16: "For God so loved the world, that he gave his only begotten Son, that whosoever believeth in him should not perish, but have everlasting life"
2. John 1:1: "In the beginning was the Word, and the Word was with God, and the Word was God"
3. John 14:6: "Jesus saith unto him, "I am the way, the truth, and the life: no man cometh unto the Father, but by me"
4. Matthew 28:19: "Go ye therefore, and teach all nations, baptizing them in the name of the Father, and of the Son, and of the Holy Ghost"
5. Romans 3:23: "For all have sinned and come short of the glory of God"
6. Ephesians 2:8: "For by grace are ye saved through faith; and that not of yourselves: it is the gift of God"
7. Genesis 1:1: "In the beginning God created the heaven and the earth"
8. Acts 1:8: "But ye shall receive power, after that the Holy Ghost is come upon you: and ye shall be witnesses unto me both in Jerusalem, and in all Judaea, and in Samaria, and unto the uttermost part of the earth"
9. 2 Timothy 3:16: "All Scripture is given by inspiration of God, and is profitable for doctrine, for reproof, for correction, for instruction in righteousness"
10. Romans 10:9: "That if thou shalt confess with thy mouth the Lord Jesus, and shalt believe in thine heart that God hath raised him from the dead, thou shalt be saved"

Chapman's website does not argue that these verses have been the most popular across history: they simply represent the most popular searches across the internet found by this particular process. The verses are mostly propositional and seem to reflect Protestant evangelical concerns in several ways, specifically the emphasis on direct action of members of the Trinity, conversion, salvation, mission and Biblical authority. There might be a suspicion therefore that the algorithm is not giving a purely historical reading or that the internet has a large body of information which reflects Protestant and post-Reformation thinking which affects the data or that it is Protestant bibliocentric (Church) organizations which are populating the internet with the right kind of material, from their viewpoint. The latter might be the case given the predominance of such 'vicarbots' – with Stephen Smith arguing that 50% of all citations on Twitter were from Bible spam accounts (Smith, 2014). Moreover, since citation of the Bible in printed books has increased dramatically over the last century simply because there are so many books being published, a current algorithmic search might only provide contemporary data with the historical data swamped by the present circumstances.

Can we dig deeper?

It is possible to use Google Ngrams to find which of these verses have been historically popular in English print culture. Google Ngrams maps word usage in specific *printed* corpora over hundreds of years, mapping the occurrence of a particular phrase (limited to five words) across the period on the *x*-axis in one or more of Google's public corpora based on printed materials (Michel et al., 2010). The methodology is being expanded at pace, especially through the Brigham Young University (BYU) Corpus Linguistics search tool (http://corpus.byu.edu), which now includes several speech-based corpora and two corpora of web-based English (NOW and GloWbE).

Neither Google Ngrams nor the BYU expansions focus specifically on social media usage. The BYU tool provides cumulative counts of actual uses across Google's various corpora for each decade in a chosen time period. I therefore input a recognizable five-word string from the King James Version (KJV) – and on occasion the New International Version (NIV)[1] – for each verse into both Google Ngrams and the BYU tool linking data to the Google Books American English Corpus of 155 billion words. I then selected the four verses with the highest frequency of occurrence in printed publications across the period 1800–2009:

1 John 3:16: 20,615 occurrences (7,126 since 1950)
2 John 1:1: 19,892 occurrences (11,499 since 1950)
3 John 14:6: 3,688 occurrences (+605 "comes to the Father" since 1840)
4 Genesis 1:1: 11,805 occurrences

I noted a discrepancy in the list in that Genesis 1:1 receives more than three times the occurrences that John 14:6, which appears four places higher in Chapman's list. However, as noted, the verses in Chapman's list represent Bible verses on the internet rather than Bible verses in printed books and also seem to reflect hermeneutical and doctrinal concerns of the contemporary Church. As such, I explored a few other verses and uncovered other popular verses:

1   Psalm 23:1: "The Lord is my Shepherd" – 14,361 occurrences
2   Matthew 7:12: "Do unto others as you would have them do to you" – 10,007 occurrences
3   Matthew 5:3: "Blessed are the poor" – 13,184 occurrences

Further research is needed to ascertain what might actually be the most popular Bible verses in the corpora across history – presumably using an alternative algorithmic process which could weight verses by frequency across a historic period? But, since this section of the research is to provide a control sample of texts showing popularity across a historically long period, a combination of these two lists provides an acceptable sample of five historically popular verses:[2]

1   John 3:16: 20,615 occurrences (7,126 since 1950)
2   John 1:1: 19,892 occurrences (11,499 since 1950)
3   Psalm 23:1: 14,361 occurrences
4   Matthew 5:3: 13,184 occurrences
5   Genesis 1:1: 11,805 occurrences

Two points stand out immediately from Figure 3.1 First, there was a major decline in use of all the verses in the period following World War One, but pre-dating the Great Depression in the 1930s. In other words, there may be wider sociological issues to pick up in the use of (at least these) Bible verses in printed culture, as there are for contemporary use of Bible

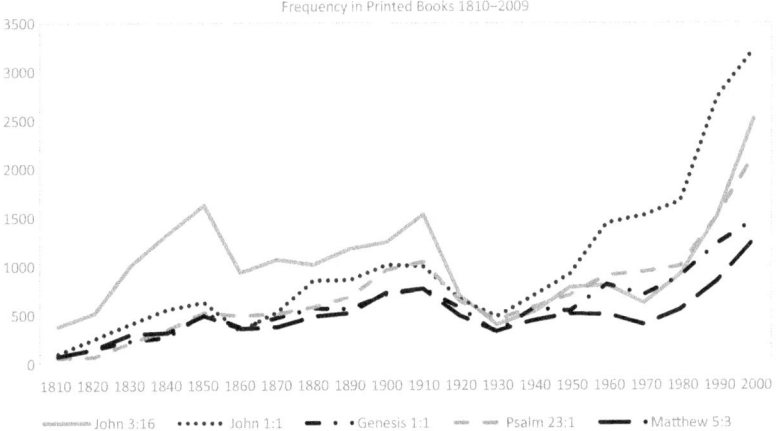

Figure 3.1 Frequency of Bible verses in print culture

verses in social media. It is noticeable that it was only in the 1980s that frequency returned to pre-war rates, but that since then the frequency of use of these Bible verses has increased remarkably, perhaps due to the rise of popular printing, church mission activities and the return of the Bible to prominence in the USA.

Notably several of these verses are propositional in character. Both of the Johannine verses, but especially John 3:16, have been used as central propositional texts outlining core incarnational theology: God intervened into the world directly through the person of Jesus Christ. Both Hebrew Bible verses offer a similar picture of a God who is directly involved in both the world and in the life of the reader: God creates (Genesis 1:1) and God (through the use of the divine name) is my Shepherd (Psalm 23:1). The latter offers a therapeutic model of Christianity in its portrayal of the pastoral aspects of the relationship between God, the author of the Psalm and, by extension, the reader. Matthew 5:3 offers a different kind of verse which does not suggest divine intervention, nor does it directly involve Jesus. As such, it models a kind of verse which, in this study, I will mark as therapeutic.

So, in one sample of frequently used texts in printed American English between 1800 and 2009, I have found a selection of texts, the most frequent of which are both propositional and Christological, but which also represent a pastoral or therapeutic approach to the Christian faith. Overall, the texts seem to be weighted towards what George Lindbeck would call a 'propositional' expression of Christianity and do not yet show a massive shift towards experiential expression or through to Lindbeck's preferred option of the cultural-linguistic expression (Lindbeck, 2002, pp. 169–195). However, it does parallel to some extent Davie's (sociology-based) shift from formal theology to informal spirituality (Davie, 2000, pp. 176–194); and, of course, Heelas and Woodhead's (theology-based) concept of the 'spiritual turn' (Heelas and Woodhead, 2005). I've noted already that these shifts are reflected in Christian Smith's exploration of millennial spirituality in his construal of MTD (Smith and Denton, 2005). But, for the time being, it is worth noticing from Figure 3.1 that my collated list suggests that therapeutic texts have been present and popular throughout the period researched and that both propositional (John 3:16) and therapeutic texts (Psalm 23:1) are increasing in frequency of citation in *printed* texts.

Step 2: create a sample of longitudinal Bible engagement in social media in English

YouVersion argues that it offers the largest free online access to multiple versions of the Bible and that its web and mobile applications allow us to interact with the Bible as we have never done before. Certainly, with downloads and installations now exceeding 300 million, *YouVersion* has made a massive impact on the use of the Bible in contemporary society. Those behind the app see that impact as directly theological:

> God is near, and so is His Word. As you wake up. While you wait. When you meet a friend. Before you go to sleep. When the Bible is always with you, it becomes a part of your daily life.
>
> (YouVersion, 2017b)

In his exploration of the use of the Bible online, Timothy Hutchings (2013, 2014) pointed to the ubiquity of *YouVersion* – although even his figures have to be recast because of subsequent growth (see also Cheong, 2014). So, the app has, by the end of 2018, been installed on over 360 million unique devices; used to read 27.2 billion chapters of the Bible; offered access to the Bible in 1,250 languages worldwide in 1,800 versions; and supported passive reading of the text, listening to the text and sharing the text (YouVersion, 2018). As the project has grown over the years, it is possible to map that growth through different figures provided in the (nearly) annual reviews provided by *YouVersion* (although different specific statistics are given in different years) (YouVersion, 2013, 2014, 2017a, 2017b, 2019). Note that the figures shown in Table 3.1 are for actions completed on the platform per se*cond*.

YouVersion's data, collected and published annually, offers a fairly robust and longitudinal data source for analyzing Bible engagement on social media, although it is not without its own limitations, as we shall see. Rather than analyze the frequency of Bible verses in published texts, these data focus on frequency of use within digital engagement and through social media. Moreover, *YouVersion*'s data can be matched with further data on social media engagement with the Bible regularly published through various other sources including *OpenBible* and *BibleGateway*, with additional control samples from the *KingJamesOnlineProject* and the *United Bible*

Table 3.1 YouVersion statistics from 2013–2018

Per Second	Installs	Bookmarks	Plans Done	Verses Shared	Audio Chapters	App Opened	Chapters Read	Highlights Created
2013		3.8		2	19	32		10
2014	1.3	3.42		2	50		314	12
2016			0.9	9	67		349	
2017	1.4		1.2	7	95	144	530	
2018				15	133		863	54

Society. Most of the lists are available online although with very little or no access to the underlying data tables.

There are two major limitations of the proposed data sources (and of the Google Ngrams data used earlier), which I decided were permissible. Firstly, I have relied upon data lists collated by the organizations rather than on the raw data figures for numbers of social media impressions (except for *OpenBible*'s two lists of most popular verses on Twitter). Since the companies involved were happy to produce the lists but were not keen to produce the raw data, I used what was available. I hope, one day, that the data will be released to academics more widely.

Secondly, the data are not categorized by age group. The figures are for engagement across all ages. As such, there is no direct correlation between the data I have for online engagement with the Bible and millennial engagement with the Bible as proposed by MTD (Smith and Denton, 2005). But then we will also see both that MTD is not only a 'youth' phenomenon and that the shift to therapeutic texts (if there is such a shift) is part of a larger trend (or re-alignment to a previous setting?) in the sociology/performance of religion. It *is* possible to argue that the data will be heavily skewed towards millennial involvement simply because they are the generation who make most use of online tools. Moreover, *YouVersion* at least is marketed heavily to the millennial market. So, in the Barna Group's *The Bible in America* report (2016a, p. 46, p. 165; see Table 3.2), figures are given for online Bible engagement.

However, in the same report, the Barna Group makes clear that the data in the report are based on "a series of telephone and online interviews with nationwide random samples" (Barna Group, 2016a, p. 167). Two of the seven sources are specifically of teenagers or millennials with the others representative across all ages. But this does not mean the data I am dealing with represent millennials – I will need to factor this limitation into the work. However, the CODEC Research Centre at Durham University have also produced a parallel piece of research in the UK which could

Table 3.2 Web engagement statistics from the Barna Group

Age Group	Web Browser	Smartphone Search	Smartphone App
Millennials (18–31 years)	75%	78%	62%
Gen Xers (32–51 years)	53%	47%	47%
Boomers (52–70 years)	42%	33%	30%
Elders (over 70 years)	21%	14%	7%

provide corroborative information, *The Bible and Digital Millennials* (Ford et al., 2019).

Having said that there is little direct quantitative data available, the numbers for the data both from *YouVersion* and *BibleGateway* are impressive. *YouVersion* lists for highlighted verses (YouVersion, 2013, 2019) range from 300 million data points in 2013 to 27.2 billion data points for 2018. *BibleGateway* (BibleGateway, 2014) argue that their data are drawn from 1.5 billion page views and 150 million unique visitors to the site in 2014, up to 1.7 billion page views and 180 million unique visitors in 2016. Moreover, for some of the *OpenBible* lists, OB14 and OB15, I have the actual number of tweets for each of the verses.

So, although I don't have specific data for each data point, if I want to explore ordinary Bible reading, then the lists drawn from *YouVersion* and *BibleGateway* data are so populous that I should be able to transcend the limitations of much smaller lists drawn from much smaller sample sizes. Since smaller lists with fewer data points might represent specialist audiences, it is possible that these huge data sets provide something closer to Jeff Astley's concept of 'ordinary' usage, namely: "the content, pattern and processes of ordinary people's articulation of their religious understanding". (2001, 56)

The lists

I explored the data in 20 different lists spread over seven years:

1 KJV12 – *KingJamesBibleOnline*'s "10 Most Popular Bible Verses of 2012" (KingJamesOnline, 2013)
2 YVP13 – *YouVersion*'s most popular Bible verses in 2013 (YouVersion, 2013; Weber, 2013)
3 BGP13 – *BibleGateway*'s top ten Bible verses searched in 2013 (Petersen, 2013)
4 YVP14 – *YouVersion*'s most popular Bible verses in 2014 (YouVersion, 2014; Zylstra, 2014)
5 YVS14 – *YouVersion*'s most shared Bible verses in 2014 (YouVersion, 2014)
6 OB14 – *OpenBible*'s "The Bible on Twitter in 2014" (Smith, 2014)
7 BGP14 – *BibleGateway*'s most popular Bible verses in 2014 (BibleGateway, 2014; Rau, 2014; Lee, 2014)
8 YVP15 – *YouVersion*'s most popular Bible verses in 2015, by country (YouVersion, 2015; Zylstra, 2015)[3]
9 OB15 – *OpenBible*'s "The Bible on Twitter in 2015" (Smith, 2015)

46 *Popular Bible verses on social media*

10 OBRT15 – *OpenBible*'s "The Bible on Twitter in 2015", most retweeted tweets (Smith, 2015)
11 BGP15 – *BibleGateway*'s most popular verses in 2015 (BibleGateway, 2015; Rau, 2015b)
12 BGA15 – *BibleGateway*'s most annotated verses in 2015 (BibleGateway, 2015)
13 YVS15 – *YouVersion*'s top shared verses of 2015 (Zylstra, 2015)
14 BGP16 – *BibleGateway*'s most popular verses in 2016 (BibleGateway, 2016)
15 BGA16 – *BibleGateway*'s most annotated, highlighted and favourited verses in 2016 (BibleGateway, 2016)
16 YVP17 – *YouVersion* most popular Bible verses in 2017 by country (YouVersion, 2017b)
17 UBS17 – *United Bible Societies* most popular verses 2017 on Digital Bible (United Bible Society, 2017)
18 BGP17 – *BibleGateway*'s most popular verses in 2017[4]
19 BGP18 – *BibleGateway*'s most popular verses in 2018 (BibleGateway, 2018)
20 YVP18 – *YouVersion*'s most popular verses in 2017. by country (YouVersion, 2019)

KJV12

1 Psalm 23:4: "Yea, though I walk through the valley of the shadow of death, I will fear no evil: for thou art with me; thy rod and thy staff they comfort me"
2 Philippians 4:13: "I can do all things through Christ which strengtheneth me"
3 John 3:16: "For God so loved the world, that he gave his only begotten Son, that whosoever believeth in him should not perish, but have everlasting life"
4 Genesis 1:1: "In the beginning God created the heaven and the earth"
5 1 Corinthians 13:11: "When I was a child, I spake as a child, I understood as a child, I thought as a child: but when I became a man, I put away childish things"
6 2 Chronicles 7:14: "If my people, which are called by my name, shall humble themselves, and pray, and seek my face, and turn from their wicked ways; then will I hear from heaven, and will forgive their sin, and will heal their land"
7 Jeremiah 29:11: "For I know the thoughts that I think toward you, saith the LORD, thoughts of peace, and not of evil, to give you an expected end"

8 Ephesians 6:12: "For we wrestle not against flesh and blood, but against principalities, against powers, against the rulers of the darkness of this world, against spiritual wickedness in high places"
9 2 Timothy 1:7: "For God hath not given us the spirit of fear; but of power, and of love, and of a sound mind"
10 Genesis 1:2: "And the earth was without form, and void; and darkness was upon the face of the deep. And the Spirit of God moved upon the face of the waters"

YVP13

1 Philippians 4:13: "I can do all this through him who gives me strength"
2 Isaiah 40:31: "But those who hope in the Lord will renew their strength. They will soar on wings like eagles; they will run and not grow weary, they will walk and not be faint"
3 Matthew 6:13: "And lead us not into temptation; but deliver us from the evil one"
4 Joshua 1:9: "Have I not commanded you? Be strong and courageous. Do not be afraid; do not be discouraged, for the Lord your God will be with you wherever you go"
5 Philippians 4:6: "Do not be anxious about anything, but in every situation, by prayer and petition, with thanksgiving, present your requests to God"

BGP13

1 John 3:16: "For God so loved the world that he gave his one and only Son, that whoever believes in him shall not perish but have eternal life"
2 Jeremiah 29:11: "'For I know the plans I have for you', declares the Lord, 'plans to prosper you and not to harm you, plans to give you hope and a future'"
3 Philippians 4:13: "I can do all this through him who gives me strength"
4 Romans 8:28: "And we know that in all things God works for the good of those who love him, who have been called according to his purpose"
5 Psalm 23: "The Lord is my shepherd, I lack nothing"
6 Proverbs 3:5–6: "Trust in the Lord with all your heart and lean not on your own understanding"
7 1 Corinthians 13:4–7: "Love is patient, love is kind. It does not envy, it does not boast, it is not proud"
8 Romans 12:2: "Do not conform to the pattern of this world, but be transformed by the renewing of your mind. Then you will be able to test and approve what God's will is – his good, pleasing and perfect will"

9 Philippians 4:6: "Do not be anxious about anything, but in every situation, by prayer and petition, with thanksgiving, present your requests to God"
10 Joshua 1:9: "Have I not commanded you? Be strong and courageous. Do not be afraid; do not be discouraged, for the Lord your God will be with you wherever you go"

YVP14

1 Romans 12:2: "Do not conform to the pattern of this world, but be transformed by the renewing of your mind. Then you will be able to test and approve what God's will is – his good, pleasing and perfect will"
2 Philippians 4:8: "Finally, brothers and sisters, whatever is true, whatever is noble, whatever is right, whatever is pure, whatever is lovely, whatever is admirable – if anything is excellent or praiseworthy – think about such things"
3 Philippians 4:6: "Do not be anxious about anything, but in every situation, by prayer and petition, with thanksgiving, present your requests to God"
4 Jeremiah 29:11: "'For I know the plans I have for you', declares the Lord, 'plans to prosper you and not to harm you, plans to give you hope and a future'"
5 Matthew 6:33: "But seek first his kingdom and his righteousness, and all these things will be given to you as well"
6 Philippians 4:7: "And the peace of God, which transcends all understanding, will guard your hearts and your minds in Christ Jesus"
7 Proverbs 3:5: "Trust in the Lord with all your heart and lean not on your own understanding"
8 Isaiah 41:10: "So do not fear, for I am with you; do not be dismayed, for I am your God. I will strengthen you and help you; I will uphold you with my righteous right hand."
9 Matthew 6:34: Therefore do not worry about tomorrow, for tomorrow will worry about itself. Each day has enough trouble of its own"
10 Proverbs 3:6: "In all your ways submit to him and he will make your paths straight"

YVS14

1 Colossians 3:23–24: "Whatever you do, work at it with all your heart, as working for the Lord, not for human masters, since you know that you will receive an inheritance from the Lord as a reward. It is the Lord Christ you are serving"

2 1 Chronicles 16:34: "Give thanks to the Lord, for he is good: his love endures forever"
3 2 Chronicles 7:14: "If my people who are called by my name will humble themselves, and pray, and seek my face"
4 Philippians 4:8: "Finally, brothers and sisters, whatever is true, whatever is noble, whatever is right, whatever is pure, whatever is lovely, whatever is admirable – if anything is excellent or praiseworthy – think about such things"
5 Jeremiah 33:2–3: "This is what the Lord says, he who made the earth, the Lord who formed it and established it – the Lord is his name: 'Call to me and I will answer you and tell you great and unsearchable things you do not know'"
6 Galatians 6:7–8: "Do not be deceived: God cannot be mocked. A man reaps what he sows. Whoever sows to please their flesh, from the flesh will reap destruction; whoever sows to please the Spirit, from the Spirit will reap eternal life"
7 Deuteronomy 6:6–7: "These commandments that I give you today are to be on your hearts. Impress them on your children. Talk about them when you sit at home and when you walk along the road, when you lie down and when you get up"
8 Romans 12:3: "For by the grace given me I say to every one of you: Do not think of yourself more highly than you ought, but rather think of yourself with sober judgment, in accordance with the faith God has distributed to each of you"
9 Psalm 103:17–18: "But from everlasting to everlasting the Lord's love is with those who fear him, and his righteousness with their children's children – with those who keep his covenant and remember to obey his precepts"

OB14

1 Philippians 4:13 (613,161): "I can do all this through him who gives me strength"
2 1 Peter 5:7 (261,417): "Cast all your anxiety on him because he cares for you"
3 Proverbs 3:5 (218,019): "Trust in the Lord with all your heart and lean not on your own understanding"
4 John 14:6 (212,883): "Jesus answered, 'I am the way and the truth and the life. No one comes to the Father except through me'"
5 John 13:7 (207,084): "Jesus replied, 'You do not realize now what I am doing, but later you will understand'"
6 1 Corinthians 13:4 (197,379): "Love is patient, love is kind. It does not envy, it does not boast, it is not proud"

7. Matthew 28:20 (187,475): "And surely I am with you always, to the very end of the age"
8. Psalm 118: 24 (183,475): "The Lord has done it this very day; let us rejoice today and be glad"
9. 2 Timothy 1:7 (182, 758): "For the Spirit God gave us does not make us timid, but gives us power, love and self-discipline"
10. Psalm 56:3 (180,139): "When I am afraid, I put my trust in you"

BGP14

1. John 3:16: "For God so loved the world that he gave his one and only Son, that whoever believes in him shall not perish but have eternal life"
2. Jeremiah 29:11: "'For I know the plans I have for you', declares the Lord, 'plans to prosper you and not to harm you, plans to give you hope and a future'"
3. Philippians 4:13: "I can do all this through him who gives me strength"
4. Romans 8:28: "And we know that in all things God works for the good of those who love him, who have been called according to his purpose"
5. Psalm 23:4: "Even though I walk through the darkest valley, I will fear no evil, for you are with me; your rod and your staff, they comfort me"
6. Philippians 4:6: "Do not be anxious about anything, but in every situation, by prayer and petition, with thanksgiving, present your requests to God"
7. 1 Corinthians 13:4: "Love is patient, love is kind. It does not envy, it does not boast, it is not proud"
8. Proverbs 3:5: "Trust in the Lord with all your heart and lean not on your own understanding"
9. 1 Corinthians 13:7: "It always protects, always trusts, always hopes, always perseveres"
10. Romans 12:2: "Do not conform to the pattern of this world, but be transformed by the renewing of your mind. Then you will be able to test and approve what God's will is – his good, pleasing and perfect will"

YVP15

x3 nations – Romans 12:2: "Do not conform to the pattern of this world, but be transformed by the renewing of your mind"

x3 nations – Joshua 1:9: "Have I not commanded you? Be strong and courageous. Do not be afraid; do not be discouraged, for the Lord your God will be with you wherever you go"

x2 nations – Jeremiah 29:11: "'For I know the plans I have for you', declares the Lord, 'plans to prosper you and not to harm you, plans to give you hope and a future'"

x1 nation – Proverbs 3:5: "Trust in the Lord with all your heart and lean not on your own understanding"
x1 nation – 1 Corinthians 10:13: "No temptation has overtaken you except what is common to mankind"
x1 nation – Philippians 4:13: "I can do all this through him who gives me strength"

OB15

1 Philippians 4:13 (262,150): "I can do all this through him who gives me strength"
2 John 3:16 (206,480): "For God so loved the world that he gave his one and only Son, that whoever believes in him shall not perish but have eternal life"
3 Jeremiah 29:11 (127,335): "'For I know the plans I have for you', declares the Lord, 'plans to prosper you and not to harm you, plans to give you hope and a future'"
4 Romans 8:18 (115,719): "For I consider that the sufferings of this present time are not worth comparing with the glory that is to be revealed to us"
5 Romans 8:28 (115,588): "And we know that for those who love God all things work together for good, for those who are called according to his purpose"
6 Proverbs 3:5 (110,216): "Trust in the Lord with all your heart and lean not on your own understanding"
7 1 Peter 5:7 (98,974): "Cast all your anxiety on him because he cares for you"
8 Romans 5:8 (97,841): "But God shows his love for us in that while we were still sinners, Christ died for us"
9 2 Timothy 1:7 (88,924): "For the Spirit God gave us does not make us timid, but gives us power, love and self-discipline"
10 Psalm 56:3 (86,998): "When I am afraid, I put my trust in you"

OBRT15

1 Philippians 1:3 (33,476 RT A@mainedcm): no text
2 1 Corinthians 13:13 (13,365 RT @allybrooke): "And now these three remain: faith, hope and love. But the greatest of these is love" #Love TrumpsAlll
3 Psalm 16:11 (11,474 RT @camerondallas): "Walk on his path and your life will be abundant" (paraphrased)
4 Romans 8:18 (10,755 RT @camerondallas): J

5 Proverbs 27:2 (10,206 RT @RealCoryMachado): paraphrased text
6 Jeremiah 29:11 (10,755 RT @ddlovato): "For I know the plans I have for you"
7 John 1:5 (7,308 RT @allybrooke): "The light shines in the darkness, and the darkness can never extinguish it"
8 Psalm 120:1 (7,550 RT @MannyPacquiaoTR): "I call on the LORD in my distress, and he answers me"
9 Colossians 3 (6,700 RT @siwonchoi): no text
10 Ephesians 4:32 (5,731 RT @TimTebow: "Be kind to one another, tender hearted, forgiving each other, just as God in Christ also has forgiven you"

BGP15

1 John 3:16: "For God so loved the world that he gave his one and only Son, that whoever believes in him shall not perish but have eternal life"
2 Jeremiah 29:11: "'For I know the plans I have for you', declares the Lord, 'plans to prosper you and not to harm you, plans to give you hope and a future'"
3 Philippians 4:13: "I can do all this through him who gives me strength"
4 Romans 8:28: "And we know that in all things God works for the good of those who love him, who have been called according to his purpose"
5 Psalm 23:4: "Even though I walk through the darkest valley, I will fear no evil, for you are with me; your rod and your staff, they comfort me"
6 Philippians 4:6: "Do not be anxious about anything, but in every situation, by prayer and petition, with thanksgiving, present your requests to God"
7 Romans 12:2: "Do not conform to the pattern of this world, but be transformed by the renewing of your mind. Then you will be able to test and approve what God's will is – his good, pleasing and perfect will"
8 Proverbs 3:5: "Trust in the Lord with all your heart and lean not on your own understanding"
9 1 Corinthians 13:7: "It always protects, always trusts, always hopes, always perseveres"
10 Proverbs 3:6: "In all your ways submit to him and he will make your paths straight"

BGA15

1 Philippians 4:6–7: "Do not be anxious about anything, but in every situation, by prayer and petition, with thanksgiving, present your requests

to God. And the peace of God, which transcends all understanding, will guard your hearts and your minds in Christ Jesus"
2. Romans 12:2: "Do not conform to the pattern of this world, but be transformed by the renewing of your mind. Then you will be able to test and approve what God's will is – his good, pleasing and perfect will"
3. Jeremiah 29:11: "'For I know the plans I have for you,' declares the Lord, 'plans to prosper you and not to harm you, plans to give you hope and a future'"
4. Proverbs 3:5–6: "Trust in the Lord with all your heart and lean not on your own understanding. In all your ways submit to him and he will make your paths straight"
5. Philippians 4:8: "Finally, brothers and sisters, whatever is true, whatever is noble, whatever is right, whatever is pure, whatever is lovely, whatever is admirable – if anything is excellent or praiseworthy – think about such things"
6. Romans 8:28: "And we know that in all things God works for the good of those who love him, who have been called according to his purpose"
7. Galatians 5:22: "But the fruit of the Spirit is love, joy, peace, forbearance, kindness, goodness, faithfulness"
8. Ephesians 6:12: "For we wrestle not against flesh and blood, but against principalities, against powers, against the rulers of the darkness of this world, against spiritual wickedness in high place"
9. Philippians 4:13: "I can do all this through him who gives me strength"
10. Matthew 6:33: "But seek first his kingdom and his righteousness, and all these things will be given to you as well"

YVS15

1. Proverbs 3:5–6: "Trust in the Lord with all your heart and lean not on your own understanding. In all your ways submit to him, and he will make your paths straight"
2. Philippians 4:6: "Do not be anxious about anything, but in every situation, by prayer and petition, with thanksgiving, present your requests to God"
3. Joshua 1:9: "Have I not commanded you? Be strong and courageous. Do not be afraid; do not be discouraged, for the Lord your God will be with you wherever you go"
4. Romans 12:2: "Do not conform to the pattern of this world, but be transformed by the renewing of your mind"
5. Romans 15:13: "May the God of hope fill you with all joy and peace as you trust in him, so that you may overflow with hope by the power of the Holy Spirit"

BGP16

1. John 3:16: "For God so loved the world that he gave his one and only Son, that whoever believes in him shall not perish but have eternal life"
2. Jeremiah 29:11: "'For I know the plans I have for you,' declares the Lord, 'plans to prosper you and not to harm you, plans to give you hope and a future'"
3. Philippians 4:13: "I can do all this through him who gives me strength"
4. Psalm 23:4: "Even though I walk through the darkest valley, I will fear no evil, for you are with me; your rod and your staff, they comfort me"
5. Romans 8:28: "And we know that in all things God works for the good of those who love him, who have been called according to his purpose"
6. Psalm 23:1: "The Lord is my shepherd, I lack nothing"
7. Psalm 23:6: "Surely your goodness and love will follow me all the days of my life, and I will dwell in the house of the Lord forever"
8. Psalm 23:5: "You prepare a table before me in the presence of my enemies. You anoint my head with oil: my cup overflows"
9. Psalm 23.3: "He refreshes my soul. He guides me along the right paths for his name's sake"
10. Philippians 4:6: "Do not be anxious about anything, but in every situation, by prayer and petition, with thanksgiving, present your requests to God"

BGA16 – top ten answers

This list has three columns ranking verses according to different social media engagement: annotation, highlighting or favouriting. In order to determine the aggregate listing, I took the position of each verse in each column and added the three figures together and ranked the verses 1–10. If a verse was not listed in a column, I added an extra 26 to the score as the original BibleGateway list gives 25 answers. Calculations are given after each verse in the aggregate list.

Aggregate

1. Philippians 4:6: "Do not be anxious about anything, but in every situation, by prayer and petition, with thanksgiving, present your requests to God" $(1 + 1 + 1 = 3)$
2. Romans 12:2: "Do not conform to the pattern of this world, but be transformed by the renewing of your mind" $(2 + 3 + 4 = 9)$
3. Philippians 4:7: "And the peace of God, which transcends all understanding, will guard your hearts and your minds in Christ Jesus" $(6 + 2 + 2 = 10)$

4 Ephesians 6:12: "For we wrestle not against flesh and blood, but against principalities, against powers, against the rulers of the darkness of this world, against spiritual wickedness in high places" (4 + 6 + 10 = 20)
5 Galatians 5:22: "But the fruit of the Spirit is love, joy, peace, forbearance, kindness, goodness, faithfulness" (5 + 7 + 9 = 21)
6 Romans 8:28: "And we know that in all things God works for the good of those who love him, who have been called according to his purpose" (11 + 5 + 5 = 21)
7 Jeremiah 29:11: "For I know the plans I have for you, declares the Lord, plans to prosper you and not to harm you, plans to give you hope and a future" (12 + 9 + 3 = 24)
8 Philippians 4:8: "Finally, brothers and sisters, whatever is true, whatever is noble, whatever is right, whatever is pure, whatever is lovely, whatever is admirable – if anything is excellent or praiseworthy – think about such things" (16 + 4 + 7 = 27)
9 Proverbs 3:5: "Trust in the Lord with all your heart and lean not on your own understanding" (20 + 8 + 6 = 34)
10 John 3:16: "For God so loved the world that he gave his one and only Son, that whoever believes in him shall not perish but have eternal life" (10 + 18 + 14 = 42)

Annotation

1 Philippians 4:6: "Do not be anxious about anything, but in every situation, by prayer and petition, with thanksgiving, present your requests to God"
2 Romans 12:2: "Do not conform to the pattern of this world, but be transformed by the renewing of your mind"
3 Romans 12:1: "Therefore, I urge you, brothers and sisters, in view of God's mercy, to offer your bodies as a living sacrifice, holy and pleasing to God – this is your true and proper worship"
4 Ephesians 6:12: "For we wrestle not against flesh and blood, but against principalities, against powers, against the rulers of the darkness of this world, against spiritual wickedness in high places"
5 Galatians 5:22: "But the fruit of the Spirit is love, joy, peace, forbearance, kindness, goodness, faithfulness"
6 Philippians 4:7: "And the peace of God, which transcends all understanding, will guard your hearts and your minds in Christ Jesus"
7 Genesis 1:1: "In the beginning God created the heavens and the earth"
8 James 1:2: "Consider it pure joy, my brothers and sisters, whenever you face trials of many kinds"
9 Hebrews 11:1: "Now faith is confidence in what we hope for and assurance about what we do not see"

10 John 3:16: "For God so loved the world that he gave his one and only Son, that whoever believes in him shall not perish but have eternal life"

Highlighting

1. Philippians 4:6: "Do not be anxious about anything, but in every situation, by prayer and petition, with thanksgiving, present your requests to God"
2. Philippians 4:7: "And the peace of God, which transcends all understanding, will guard your hearts and your minds in Christ Jesus"
3. Romans 12:2: "Do not conform to the pattern of this world, but be transformed by the renewing of your mind"
4. Philippians 4:8: "Finally, brothers and sisters, whatever is true, whatever is noble, whatever is right, whatever is pure, whatever is lovely, whatever is admirable – if anything is excellent or praiseworthy – think about such things"
5. Romans 8:28: "And we know that in all things God works for the good of those who love him, who have been called according to his purpose"
6. Ephesians 6:12: "For we wrestle not against flesh and blood, but against principalities, against powers, against the rulers of the darkness of this world, against spiritual wickedness in high places"
7. Galatians 5:22: "But the fruit of the Spirit is love, joy, peace, forbearance, kindness, goodness, faithfulness"
8. Proverbs 3:5: "Trust in the Lord with all your heart and lean not on your own understanding"
9. Jeremiah 29:11: "'For I know the plans I have for you', declares the Lord, 'plans to prosper you and not to harm you, plans to give you hope and a future'"
10. Ephesians 2:8: "For it is by grace you have been saved, through faith – and this is not from yourselves, it is the gift of God"

Favouriting

1. Philippians 4:6: "Do not be anxious about anything, but in every situation, by prayer and petition, with thanksgiving, present your requests to God"
2. Philippians 4:7: "And the peace of God, which transcends all understanding, will guard your hearts and your minds in Christ Jesus"
3. Jeremiah 29:11: "'For I know the plans I have for you', declares the Lord, 'plans to prosper you and not to harm you, plans to give you hope and a future'"
4. Romans 12:2: "Do not conform to the pattern of this world, but be transformed by the renewing of your mind"

5 Romans 8:28: "And we know that in all things God works for the good of those who love him, who have been called according to his purpose"
6 Proverbs 3:5: "Trust in the Lord with all your heart and lean not on your own understanding"
7 Philippians 4:8: "Finally, brothers and sisters, whatever is true, whatever is noble, whatever is right, whatever is pure, whatever is lovely, whatever is admirable – if anything is excellent or praiseworthy – think about such things"
8 Philippians 4:13: "I can do all this through him who gives me strength"
9 Galatians 5:22: "But the fruit of the Spirit is love, joy, peace, forbearance, kindness, goodness, faithfulness"
10 Ephesians 6:12: "For we wrestle not against flesh and blood, but against principalities, against powers, against the rulers of the darkness of this world, against spiritual wickedness in high places"

YVP17

x17 nations – Joshua 1:9: "Have I not commanded you? Be strong and courageous. Do not be afraid; do not be discouraged, for the Lord your God will be with you wherever you go"

x10 nations – Jeremiah 29:11: "For I know the plans I have for you', declares the Lord, 'plans to prosper you and not to harm you, plans to give you hope and a future'"

x5 nations – John 3:16: "For God so loved the world that he gave his one and only Son, that whoever believes in him shall not perish but have eternal life"

x4 nations – Romans 8:28: "And we know that in all things God works for the good of those who love him, who have been called according to his purpose"

x1 nation – Romans 12:2: "Let your hope keep you joyful, be patient in your troubles, and pray at all times"

x1 nation – 2 Timothy 1:7: "For God hath not given us the spirit of fear; but of power, and of love, and of a sound mind"

x1 nationvPsalm 119: "Blessed are they whose ways are blameless, who walk according to the law of the Lord"

x1 nation – Romans 12:3: "For by the grace given me I say to every one of you: Do not think of yourself more highly than you ought, but rather think of yourself with sober judgment, in accordance with the faith God has distributed to each of you"

x1 nation – Corinthians 10:3: "They all ate the same spiritual food"

x1 nation – Colossians 3: "Since, then, you have been raised with Christ, set your hearts on things above, where Christ is, seated at the right hand of God" x1 nation – Proverbs 16:9: "In their hearts humans plan their course, but the Lord establishes their steps"

x1 nation – 2 Corinthians 12:9: "But he said to me, 'My grace is sufficient for you, for my power is made perfect in weakness'"

UBS17

1 Isaiah 43:1–2: "Israel, the Lord who created you says, Do not be afraid – I will save you. I have called you by name – you are mine. When you pass through deep waters, I will be with you; your troubles will not overwhelm you"
2 Jeremiah 32:27: "I am the Lord, the God of all people. Nothing is too difficult for me"
3 Mark 11:24: "For this reason, I tell you: When you pray and ask for something, believe that you have received it, and you will be given whatever you ask for"
4 Psalm 71:5: "Sovereign Lord, I put my hope in you; I have trusted in you since I was young"
5 Romans 12:12: "Let your hope keep you joyful, be patient in your troubles, and pray at all times"
6 Jeremiah 17:7–8: "But I will bless the person, who puts his trust in me. He is like a tree growing near a stream and sending out roots to the water"
7 Psalm 30:5: "His anger lasts only a moment, his goodness for a lifetime. Tears may flow in the night, but joy comes in the morning"
8 Ecclesiastes 3:11: "He has set the right time for everything. He has given us a desire to know the future, but never gives us the satisfaction of fully understanding what he does"
9 Psalm 56:3: "When I am afraid, O Lord, I put my trust in you"
10 Psalm 34:18: "The Lord is near to those who are discouraged; he saves those who have lost all hope"

BGP17

1 John 3:16: "For God so loved the world that he gave his one and only Son, that whoever believes in him shall not perish but have eternal life"
2   Jeremiah 29:11: "'For I know the plans I have for you', declares the Lord, 'plans to prosper you and not to harm you, plans to give you hope and a future'"
3 Philippians 4:13: "I can do all this through him who gives me strength"
4 Romans 8:28: "And we know that in all things God works for the good of those who love him, who have been called according to his purpose"

5   Psalm 23:4: "Even though I walk through the darkest valley, I will fear no evil, for you are with me; your rod and your staff, they comfort me"
6   Romans 12:2: "Do not conform to the pattern of this world, but be transformed by the renewing of your mind"
7   Philippians 4:6: "Do not be anxious about anything, but in every situation, by prayer and petition, with thanksgiving, present your requests to God"
8   Psalm 23:1: "The Lord is my shepherd, I lack nothing"
9   Joshua 1:9: "Have I not commanded you? Be strong and courageous. Do not be afraid; do not be discouraged, for the Lord your God will be with you wherever you go"
10 Psalm 23:6: "Surely your goodness and love will follow me all the days of my life, and I will dwell in the house of the Lord forever"

BGP18

1   Jeremiah 29:11: "'For I know the plans I have for you', declares the Lord, 'plans to prosper you and not to harm you, plans to give you hope and a future"
2   John 3:16: "For God so loved the world that he gave his one and only Son, that whoever believes in him shall not perish but have eternal life"
3   Philippians 4:13: "I can do all this through him who gives me strength"
4   Romans 8:28: "And we know that in all things God works for the good of those who love him, who have been called according to his purpose"
5   Psalm 23:4: "Even though I walk through the darkest valley, I will fear no evil, for you are with me; your rod and your staff, they comfort me"
6   Romans 12:2: "Do not conform to the pattern of this world, but be transformed by the renewing of your mind"
7   Psalm 23:6: "Surely your goodness and love will follow me all the days of my life, and I will dwell in the house of the Lord forever"
8   Psalm 23:1: "The Lord is my shepherd, I lack nothing"
9   Psalm 23:5: "You prepare a table before me in the presence of my enemies. You anoint my head with oil: my cup overflows"
10 Matthew 6:33: "But seek first his kingdom and his righteousness, and all these things will be given to you as well"

YVP18

x10 nations – Jeremiah 29:11: "For I know the plans I have for you, declares the Lord, plans to prosper you and not to harm you, plans to give you hope and a future" x8 nations – Isaiah 41:10: "So do not fear, for I am with you; do not be dismayed, for I am your God. I will strengthen you and help you; I will uphold you with my righteous right hand"

x5 nations – Joshua 1:9: "Have I not commanded you? Be strong and courageous. Do not be afraid; do not be discouraged, for the Lord your God will be with you wherever you go"

x3 nations – John 3:16: "For God so loved the world that he gave his one and only Son, that whoever believes in him shall not perish but have eternal life"

x3 nations – 1 Peter 5:7: "Cast all your anxiety on him because he cares for you"

x2 nations – Matthew 6:33: "But seek first his kingdom and his righteousness, and all these things will be given to you as well"

x2 nations – Proverbs 4:23: "Above all else, guard your heart, for everything you do flows from it"

x1 nation – Proverbs 16:9: "In their hearts humans plan their course, but the Lord establishes their steps"

x1 nation – Romans 8:28: And we know that in all things God works for the good of those who love him, who have been called according to his purpose.

Aggregating the lists

I will refer back to the specific lists, or groups of them, in my reflections, but I present here, in Table 3.3, an aggregation of all the data sorted by the frequency of occurrence across all 20 lists. I feel that this chart is helpful to see the data more easily. I limited this list to those verses which have appeared more than three times across the 20 lists. Lists beginning with the letters *BG* are drawn from the *BibleGateway* website and *YV* from data provided by the *YouVersion* Bible app. I further condensed this data into a list of the top 12 verses – those verses which appeared four or more times across all 20 lists.

The aggregate list of the top 12 popular Bible verses from 2012–2019

1. Jeremiah 29:11: "'For I know the plans I have for you', declares the Lord, "plans to prosper you and not to harm you, plans to give you hope and a future"
2. Philippians 4:13: "I can do all this through him who gives me strength"
3. Romans 12:2: "Do not conform to the pattern of this world; but be transformed by the renewing of your mind"

Table 3.3 The aggregate list

Bible Verses	KJV12	YVP13	BGP13	YVP14	YVS14	OB14	BGP14	YVP15	OB15	OBRT15	BGP15	BGA15	YVS15	BGP16	BGA16 (Agg)	YVP17	UBS17	BGP17	BGP18	YVP18	Σ
Jeremiah 29:11	7						2	x2 nations	3	6	2	3		2	24	x10 nations		2	1	x10 nation	15
Philippians 4:13	2	1	3			1	3	x1 nation	1		3	9		3	47			3	3		13
Romans 12:2			8	1			10	x3 nation			7	2	4		9	x1 nation	5	6	6		12
John 3:16	3		1				1		2		1			1	42	x5 nation		1	2	x3 nation	11
Romans 8:28			4				4		5		4	6		5	21	x4 nation		4	4	x1 nation	11
Philippians 4:6		5	9	3, 6			6				6	1	2	10	3			7			10
Proverbs 3:5			6	7, 10		3	8	x1 nation	6		8	4	1		34						10
Psalm 23:4	1		5				5				5			4				5	5	x5 nation	7
Joshua 1:9		4	10					x3 nation					3			x17 nations		9			7
2 Timothy 1:7	9					9			9							x1 nation					4
Philippians 4:8				2								5			27						4
Matthew 6:33				5	4							10							10	x2 nation	4
Psalm 23:6														7				10	7		3
Psalm 23:1														6				8	8		3
Psalm 56:3						10			10								9				3
Ephesians 6:12	8											8			20						3
1 Corinthians 13:4			7			6	7														3
1 Peter 5:7						2			7											x3 nation	3

4   John 3:16: "For God so loved the world that he gave his one and only Son, that whoever believes in him shall not perish but have eternal life"
5   Romans 8:28: "And we know that in all things God works for the good of those who love him, who have been called according to his purpose"
6   Philippians 4:6: "Do not be anxious about anything, but in every situation, by prayer and petition, with thanksgiving, present your requests to God"
7   Proverbs 3:5: "Trust in the Lord with all your heart and lean not on your own understanding"
8   Psalm 23:4: "Even though I walk through the darkest valley, I will fear no evil, for you are with me; your rod and your staff, they comfort me"
9   Joshua 1:9: "Have I not commanded you? Be strong and courageous. Do not be afraid; do not be discouraged, for the Lord your God will be with you wherever you go"
10 2 Timothy 1:7: "For God hath not given us the spirit of fear; but of power, and of love, and of a sound mind"
11 Philippians 4:8: "Finally, brothers and sisters, whatever is true, whatever is noble, whatever is right, whatever is pure, whatever is lovely, whatever is admirable – if anything is excellent or praiseworthy – think about such things"
12 Matthew 6:33: "But seek first his kingdom and his righteousness, and all these things will be given to you as well"

The aggregate table (Table 3.3) brings together lots of data drawn from lots of different data sources. Most of those lists do not provide the specific data count for each verse but instead provide a simple hierarchy of verses. Occasionally, the data have been released or are retrievable (*OpenBible* OB14, OB15, OBRT15). I have noted that many of the other lists, especially those from Bible *Gateway* and *YouVersion*, are based on large amounts of data representing billions of searches or hundreds of millions of social media engagements. Had I the quantitative data, I could have found that different lists are more significant than others in terms of the specific frequency of occurrences of specific verses; however, the complexities of retrieving the data for every list or for retrieving the data from Google Analytics or algorithmic searches would be prohibitively expensive in terms of both time and money. Moreover, I am aware that the data provided do not differentiate between the languages of Bible versions used: everything is recorded as though it were read/engaged in English.

I will explore both the aggregate list and the other 20 lists, or groups of them, in Chapter 4. When exploring these lists, I will be looking at a number of relatively specific questions rather than going through each list in turn and answer similar questions repeatedly.

Notes

1 I made use of alternative translations where there was a significant shift of language when new translations were introduced which clearly changed the wording for the verse in such a way that the KJV wording became obsolete.
2 Note that these figures are dwarfed in subsequent online lists: for example, the number of times Bible verses are tweeted in OB14 and OB15.
3 *YouVersion* (2015) provides data for the most popular Bible verse of all time by country. Slightly different data are provided (the most popular Bible verses in 2015 by country) in the summary and infographic produced in Zylstra (2015); these data are used in this book.
4 *BibleGateway* did not release these data publicly, but the list was made available to me through private correspondence with *BibleGateway*'s Chief Data Analyst, Stephen Smith.

4 Analysis/reflection

This chapter offers some analysis and reflection on the data presented in the last chapter. To avoid unnecessary repetition and keep the argument succinct, the lists have been put into distinct groups – normally by mode of engagement, but also by Digital Bible platforms. So, in the following sections, I look at groups of lists – the YVP, BGP, BGA, YVS and OB series – and then look across all the lists together. The 20 lists include a total of 79 Bible verses drawn from the Hebrew Bible/Old Testament (37) and the New Testament (42). However, the aggregate list of the top 12 verses across all the lists includes eight verses from the New Testament and four from the Hebrew Bible, showing a concentration of New Testament texts in the list of more popular texts.

1. YVP13, YVP14, YVP15, YVP17, YVP18

The YVP lists (YouVersion 2013, 2014, 2015, 2017b, 2019) include the most popular verses across the *YouVersion* site/platform across the last six years – including bookmarks, highlights and shares. They both resemble yet differ from the series of lists compiled by *BibleGateway* (BGP13–18) during the same period. In 2013 and 2014, the lists were simply of Bible verses in order of popularity. At the end of 2015, *YouVersion* published summary data on the use of their app which included data on the most popular verses by country (YouVersion, 2015). These data reappear in a slightly different form in *Christianity Today's* summary giving popularity by country for 2015 (Zylstra, 2015). In *YouVersion's* reviews of 2017 and 2018, similar lists of popular verses by country were produced (YouVersion 2017b, 2019). Table 4.1 brings this series of lists together and also includes a process of aggregating the verses (the column headed $\sum$) so that the most popular verses across the five lists appear towards the top of the table. This is almost essential since the lists in the first couple of years bore little resemblance to each other (later I note the same lack of continuity between YVS14 and YVS15). Conformity came with time, which is itself an interesting point.

Table 4.1 YVP13–18

2013 (YVP2013)	2014 (YVP2014)	2015 (YVP2015)	2017 (YVP17)	2018 (YVP18)	Σ	Verses
4		Mexico, Colombia, Brazil	Argentina, Brazil, Chile, Colombia, Costa Rica, Dominican Republic, Ecuador, Egypt, France, Germany, Guatemala, Italy, Mexico, Netherlands, Peru, Spain, Venezuela	Argentina, Brazil, Colombia, Germany, Mexico.	4	Joshua 1:9: "Have I not commanded you? Be strong and courageous. Do not be afraid; do not be discouraged, for the Lord your God will be with you wherever you go".
	4	Nigeria, South Africa	Canada, Indonesia, Malaysia, Philippines, Singapore Japan, Kenya, Nigeria, South Africa, UK	Australia, Canada, Ghana, Indonesia, Japan, Nigeria, Philippines, Singapore, UAE, UK	4	Jeremiah 29:11: "'For I know the plans I have for you', declares the Lord, 'plans to prosper you and not to harm you, plans to give you hope and a future'".
	1	USA, Canada, UK	Australia		3	Romans 12:2: "Do not conform to the pattern of this world, but be transformed by the renewing of your mind".
1		South Korea			2	Philippians 4:13: "I can do all this through him who gives me strength".
5	3				2	Philippians 4:6: "Do not be anxious about anything, but in every situation, by prayer and petition, with thanksgiving, present your requests to God".
	5			Thailand, Vietnam	2	Matthew 6:33: "But seek first his kingdom and his righteousness, and all these things will be given to you as well".

(Continued)

Table 4.1 (Continued)

2013 (YVP2013)	2014 (YVP2014)	2015 (YVP2015)	2017 (YVP17)	2018 (YVP18)	Σ	Verses
	7	Australia			2	Proverbs 3:5: "Trust in the Lord with all your heart and lean not on your own understanding."
	8			Chile, France, Italy, Netherlands, Peru, South Africa, Spain, USA	2	Isaiah 41:10: "So do not fear, for I am with you; do not be dismayed, for I am your God. I will strengthen you and help you; I will uphold you with my righteous right hand".
			Cambodia, Vietnam, Thailand, India, Ghana	Bangladesh, Nepal, Turkey	2	John 3:16: "For God so loved the world that he gave his one and only son, that whoever believes in him shall not perish but have eternal life".
			USA, Russia, Romania, Taiwan	Ukraine	2	Romans 8:28: "And we know that in all things God works for the good of those who love him".
		China	China		2	1 Corinthians 10:13: "No temptation has overtaken you except what is common to humankind".

2013 (YVP2013)	2014 (YVP2014)	2015 (YVP2015)	2017 (YVP17)	2018 (YVP18)	Σ	Verses
			South Korea	South Korea	2	Proverbs 16:9: "In their hearts, humans plan their course, but the Lord establishes their steps".
2					1	Isaiah 40:31: "But those who hope in the Lord will renew their strength. They will soar on wings like eagles".
3					1	Matthew 6:13: "And lead us not into temptation; but deliver us from the evil one".
	2				1	Philippians 4:8: "Finally, brothers and sisters, whatever is true, whatever is noble, whatever is right, whatever is pure"
	6				1	Philippians 4:7: "And the peace of God, which transcends all understanding"
	9				1	Matthew 6:34: "Therefore, do not worry about tomorrow, for tomorrow will worry about itself".
	10				1	Proverbs 3:6: "In all your ways submit to him, and he will make your paths straight".
				Egypt, India, Iraq	1	1 Peter 5:7: "Cast all your anxiety on him because he cares for you".
				China, Russia	1	Proverbs 4:23: "Above all else, guard your heart, for everything you do flows from it".

As noted already, these lists represent all Bible engagement across the *YouVersion* platform (bookmarks, highlights and shares), representing large amounts of data from across the world, across different cultures, genders and ages. Bible engagement online is itself an area of ongoing research. So, in his exploration of screen reading vs. paper reading, Ziming Liu referred to differences in levels of engagement with texts which seemed to be linked to screen engagement and/or paper engagement (Liu, 2008). He referred to those differences in terms of 'extensive' or 'intensive' reading; I have used the same language when reflecting on the work done by Louise Rosenblatt, Stanislas Dehaene (2009) and Mary Wolf (2008). (see also Baron, 2015; Phillips, 2018). In this discussion, then, the performance of Bible engagement will be explored as a kind of scale from extensive (light, searching, passive) to intensive (deep, sharing, active) engagement.

Some later lists will need to be classed as representing intensive engagement, especially those giving data on verses shared (YVS14–15), tweeted (OB14–15) or annotated (BGA15–16). In addition, some lists – particularly the BGP-prefixed lists – record more extensive engagement (searching, reading, listening). Extensive engagement might be classified as the consumption of the Bible since it focuses on people gaining information about the Bible or reading/listening to the Bible online. Such engagement isn't really viewed by an audience external to the consumer, except through data gathering by the Bible platforms. More intense forms of engagement, especially on platforms such as *YouVersion* which encourage users to open up their activity to review by a peer group, are part and parcel of a more active, participatory performance of Bible engagement: Bible engagement as performance. To some extent, *YouVersion* social network developments have clouded the difference, since now users' friends can also see their reading patterns and users can share plans with others (Hutchings, 2017a).

So, while the various groups of lists allow me to separate out consumption of the Bible (BGP) and active distribution of Bible verses (YVS, OB), these YVP verses sit somewhere in the middle, with users engaged in consumption of the Bible, in personal (private) annotation (highlighting, bookmarking), as well as in publicly sharing Bible verses. In 2014 and 2015, consumption of the Bible on the *YouVersion* platform dwarfed the number of verses shared: 314 chapters were read every second, with two verses shared every second. As such, the YVP lists should almost certainly be seen as reflecting extensive engagement (consumption) rather than intensive engagement.

Remember that in print culture, John 3:16 remains one of the most common verses. Indeed, it remains extremely popular even on social media, as will be seen in the BGP series of lists. But wherever the lists focus on more intensive engagement with the text, John 3:16 tends to disappear from the top of the lists. When Sarah Zylstra (2014) wrote an article about this list for

Christianity Today, the headline made note of the absence: "Sorry Again, John 3:16: The World's 10 Most Popular Bible Verses of 2014", which refers back to a previous article (Steffan, 2013) and other Bible lists in which John 3:16 was also absent. In fact, the articles note the differences between *YouVersion*'s lists and those on *BibleGateway*. Those differences may well reflect different types of users (fewer millennials on *BibleGateway*?) or the affordances of different platforms, since *BibleGateway* is seen more as a 'desktop' platform and *YouVersion* as a mobile platform. But it may also be a sign that different verses are found in lists of extensive engagement than those found in lists of intensive engagement. So, I will note the series of BGP lists where John 3:16 remains the most popular verse through to 2018. The BGP lists represent the most extensive engagement (searching, consuming) of all the lists on the most extensive platform (*BibleGateway*).

Indeed, this process can be demonstrated in a simple exercise. I conducted a simple Google search for John 3:16 and found that in the results *BibleGateway* appeared in the top three slots, with no sign of *YouVersion* within the top ten *pages* of results.[1] Since most people click on the top results, then this means that more extensive engagement (searching, consuming) is more likely to be evidenced in the BGP lists rather than in the YVP lists.

Moreover, this also suggests that engagement on the *YouVersion* lists tends to reflect more intensive social performance of Bible engagement. In CODEC's work on the Bible and Digital Millennials (Ford et al., 2019), corroborated by the Barna Group's research into Digital Millennial attitudes (Barna Group, 2015, 2016a), I noted a tendency for Bible-centric millennials to engage more intensively with the Bible (Ford et al., 2019; Phillips, 2017, 2018), while those who were less Bible-centric to engage more extensively. So, the former preferred paper Bibles, Bible study and Bible devotion while the latter preferred Bible searching, passage look-up and reading. However, I also noted that this group of Bible-centric Digital Millennials were much less likely to share the Bible online (they preferred to do this offline) than other groups of less Bible-centric Christian Digital Millennials. I need to note that this exploration of the social performance of Bible engagement is limited in its focus on online lists and should not be taken as a complete and exhaustive exploration of Bible engagement in contemporary culture.

The majority of the verses in the YVP series of lists (as shown in the aggregate list in Chapter 3; see Table 3.3) are what might call broadly be called 'therapeutic' verses. In other words, they represent what Abby Day (2010, p. 11) called 'anthropocentric' or 'practice-centred' faith rather than a 'theocentric' or 'propositional' approach to faith: the verses reflect the kind of faith users have found efficacious in their everyday experience of lived religion rather than verses which reflect the doctrinal/creedal propositions of the religion/Church.

To some extent John 3:16 is a good example of the latter and Philippians 4:13 a good example of the former. John 3:16 states God's activity of sending his son to express his love for the world and the offer of salvation based on belief in this activity. God is the verbal subject and the verse makes direct reference to the ministry of Jesus and states that salvation is dependent on (creedal/theocentric) belief (Day, 2011, pp. 156–158). Philippians 4:13, in contrast, is written in the first person (so in the voice of the author, or the [re]tweeter?) and offers a general statement of confidence to complete a task "through him" who has given strength to me. Because of subject transference in sharing this verse – as in retweeting discussed in at the end of Chapter 2 (Murthy, 2013, p. 45) – the user both identifies with and co-opts the author's sentiment as their own; the user joins the author in stating their inner confidence "through him" who has given strength. But the verse does not mention who "he" might be. God is not referenced; Jesus is not referenced. Instead the verse becomes a therapeutic aphorism. Indeed, the list shows both the popularity of Philippians 4 but also the fragmentation of Philippians 4. Evidently, this is because Bible verses are easily captured as data segments and are also the right length to be tweeted/shared and as such all Bible chapters tend to be fragmented into verses. Jeffrey Siker (2017, p. 197) and John Weaver (2017b) have both raised the problem of fragmentation and loss of context. But I note, as seen in the fragmentation of Philippians 4, the verses which tend to appear in the popular verse lists are the 'therapeutic' verses which tend to avoid mention of God or Jesus and which focus on the internal attitude of the speaker or the addressee (Philippians 4:6, 4:8, 4:13). Philippians 4:7, for example, is found in only one list (YPV14) and mentions both God and Christ Jesus, but again the thrust of the verse is about the therapeutic impact of God's peace on the addressee.

So, most of the popular verses in this group of lists reflect the psychological need to deal with personal anxiety and security rather than focus on the externalization of that faith in propositional statements. The human subject is central. Several of the verses represent Paul's reflections on theological transformation of our minds, which, he proposes, have a beneficial effect on our attitudes and behaviour (Romans 12, Philippians 4). Indeed, the top three verses in YVP15 (Proverbs 3:5–6, Philippians 4:6–7 and Joshua 1:9), all continue the trend in that direction. God's agency in these texts seems minimal or passive. The verses call for our minds to be transformed so that we can discern what is God's will (Romans 12:2); for us to be strong and courageous as commanded by God, who is with us wherever we go (Joshua 1:9).

So, the social performance of Bible engagement presented in this group of lists is one which resonates closely with Day's concept of performative belief. Indeed, the group of lists provides a classic example of what Christian Smith would call 'moralistic therapeutic deism' (MTD) (Smith and Denton, 2005; see the next chapter): God is a bystander to the project, the always present Divine Butler, who has set things in motion and then stands by as individuals sort out their own lives by transforming their own minds. In other words, individuals are the centre of the therapeutic move – what they choose to focus on matters rather than on what God has done or how God/Jesus/the Spirit has intervened. I note this in other verses in the list: the call to be strong and courageous (Joshua 1:9), to seek first the kingdom of God (Matthew 6:33), to trust in God with all our heart (Proverbs 3:5) and to acknowledge God in all our ways (Proverbs 3:6). All of these verses point to the self-therapeutic activity of the faithful individual rather than to an active role for the divine.

Some of the verses do represent God as addressing the reader/addressee or as the verbal subject of the verse: Joshua 1:9, Jeremiah 29:11, Proverbs 3:5 (?), Isaiah 41:10, John 3:16, Romans 8:28, Proverbs 16:9 and so on. But the agency of God is relatively muted compared to John 3:16, often amounting to abiding presence rather direct intervention in people's daily lives (Joshua 1:9, Proverbs 3:5, Isaiah 41:10). Indeed, in Joshua 1:9, God seems to command a therapeutic, practice-based attitude to faith based on his abiding presence.

It is worth looking at Jeremiah 29:11 in a bit more detail, not least because this verse grows in popularity across the whole list of verses and stands at the very top of the aggregate list. The verse appears four times across the five YVP lists and is listed as one of the most popular verses in a large group of countries in both the Global South and the Global North in 2017 and 2018. But its popularity within wider Christianity has been somewhat controversial. Thomas Turner (2014) talks of the verse being "doled out like a doctor explaining a prescription: *Take Jeremiah 29:11 a few times, with a full glass of water, and call me in the morning. I think you'll feel better*". Turner's argument, of course, is that the verse is spoken as part of a letter to the Jewish people who are in exile in Babylon (Jeremiah 29:4). As various commentators point out (Keown, Scalise and Smothers, 1995, pp. 71–73; Lundbom, 2004, pp. 353–354, pp. 359–360; Stulman, 2005, pp. 249–257), this verse has a specific context in the life of the exiled Jews and says that God does have plans for them, despite all that they are going through. However, the return to security in Jerusalem lies not in the near future but in 70 years, when most of those sent into exile will have died (Jeremiah 27:9, 28:11). God has plans that all will be well – the most welcome of plans for those in anxiety and fear, palpably therapeutic – but such plans are to be delayed until his people have learnt the lessons of exile and will bypass at least two generations, only then in 70 years, will they be ready to return

72 *Analysis/reflection*

to Jerusalem. As Turner and others have noted, however, in contemporary usage the verse acts as a kind of amulet of protection – a verse of utter hopefulness that God has a plan to sort everything out to our benefit: all will be well and it will be well because God intends it to be so. But the details of the plan like the details of the problem are erased through the decontextualization of the verse. The verse is radically individualized, radically generalized, to match any therapeutic agenda which might be thrown at it.

Interestingly, this use of Jeremiah 29:11 unpicks Day's concept of practice-based performative belief. Though the verse may be generally true from hindsight (God did have plans and all works out relatively well, or will do in the end), it is hard to make this verse fit every specific situation and every specific problem. The verse, in context, is about a specific issue for which God, presumably, had specific plans. It is not a panacea for all problems. Indeed, there is a story of a senior youth leader offering a session at a festival entitled "When Jeremiah 29:11 doesn't work out", and the venue being filled three times over. Whilst the other verses are about therapeutic change *now*, Jeremiah 29:11 is about *the future*, about plans God has for us. So, the verse is about the hope that God has got plans and will sort it out for our benefit, for us to prosper. Of course, this might be part of a prosperity doctrine too, that with God we will prosper financially. The hope of therapy, the promise that God is a God of prosperity, a God of hope and a God of the future, are clearly popular themes for people to bookmark, highlight and share.

2. BGP13–18

BibleGateway publishes an annual review of data from their site and has offered a list of popular verses for six of these reports from 2013 to 2018 (Petersen, 2013; BibleGateway, 2014, 2015, 2016, 2018). *BibleGateway* did not publicly release data for 2017, but the list was made available for this research through private correspondence with *BibleGateway*'s Chief Data Analyst, Stephen Smith. As early as 2013, the data were drawn from 456 million visits resulting in 1.5 billion views (Petersen, 2013) and in 2016 1.7 billion page views from more than 180 million unique visitors from across the world. The data were not differentiated by age or gender. Table 4.2 summarizes the most popular verses in the lists.

BibleGateway's data in these lists are drawn solely from data for searches (stated in Petersen, 2013 but assumed for the other years since the format remains consistent). This means that it differs from the *YouVersion* lists discussed, which focussed on bookmarking, highlighting and sharing. This list relates to the more extensive form of Bible engagement (searching, consuming).

Table 4.2 BGP13–18

2013 (BGP13)	2014 (BGP14)	2015 (BGP15)	2016 (BGP16)	2017 (BGP17)	2018 (BGP18)	Σ	Verses
2	2	2	2	2	1	6	Jeremiah 29:11: "'For I know the plans I have for you', declares the Lord, 'plans to prosper you and not to harm you, plans to give you hope and a future'".
1	1	1	1	1	2	6	John 3:16: "For God so loved the world that he gave his one and only son, that whoever believes in him shall not perish but have eternal life".
3	3	3	3	3	3	6	Philippians 4:13: "I can do all this through him who gives me strength".
4	4	4	5	4	4	6	Romans 8:28: "And we know that in all things God works for the good of those who love him".
5	5	5	4	5	5	6	Psalm 23:4: "Even though I walk through the darkest valley, I will fear no evil, for you are with me; your rod and your staff, they comfort me".
8	10	7		6	6	5	Romans 12:2: "Do not conform to the pattern of this world; but be transformed by the renewing of your mind".
9	6	6	10	7		5	Philippians 4:6: "Do not be anxious about anything, but in every situation, by prayer and petition, with thanksgiving, present your requests to God".
6	8	8				3	Proverbs 3:5: "Trust in the Lord with all your heart and lean not on your own understanding".
			7	10	7	3	Psalm 23:6: "Surely your goodness and love will follow me all the days of my life, and I will dwell in the house of the Lord forever".
			6	8	8	3	Psalm 23:1: "The Lord is my shepherd, I lack nothing".
10				9		2	Joshua 1:9: "Have I not commanded you? Be strong and courageous. Do not be afraid; do not be discouraged, for the Lord your God will be with you wherever you go".
7	7					2	1 Corinthians 13:4: "Love is patient, love is kind. It does not envy, it does not boast, it is not proud".
			8		9	2	Psalm 23:5: "You prepare a table before me in the presence of my enemies. You anoint my head with oil; my cup overflows".
	9	9				2	1 Corinthians 13:7: "It always protects, always trusts, always hopes, always perseveres".
					10	1	Matthew 6:33: "But seek first his kingdom and his righteousness, and all these things will be given to you as well".
			9			1	Psalm 23:3: "He refreshes my soul. He guides me along the right paths for his name's sake".

74 Analysis/reflection

This is the most prolonged series of reports, providing the most internally consistent set of data. We see at the top of Figure 4.1 what will become the perennial favourites (John 3:16, Jeremiah 29:11 and Philippians 4:13), and we note the final shift of Jeremiah 29:11 into the top spot in BGP18. Further down the list, that consistency is fractured by verses moving in and out of the top 12.

Interestingly, Joshua 1:9, *YouVersion*'s verse of the year for 2017, registers at ninth in the BGP17 list and appears elsewhere in 2013 at tenth position. In other words, the different platforms present different data. The Bible engagement which made Joshua 1:9 the verse of the year on *YouVersion* was not replicated on *BibleGateway*. This could be that *YouVersion* is promoting specific verses across its own platform, although the geographic spread of this verse's popularity seems to argue against this. Indeed, this may be the precise issue: the multilingual availability of *YouVersion* and the spread of versions in other languages than English is impressive. Whilst *BibleGateway* offers a similar spread of versions, the site feels Anglophone. So, when Joshua 1:9 becomes the most popular verse on *YouVersion*, that

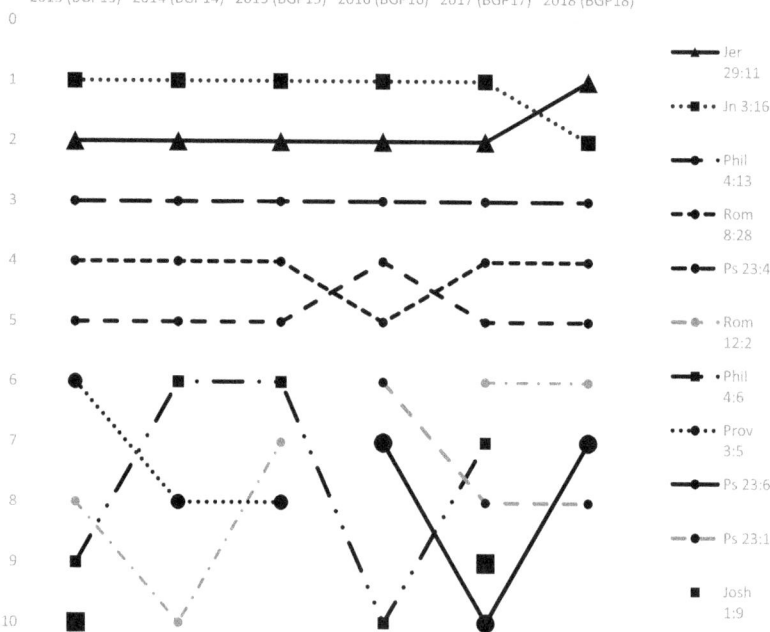

Figure 4.1 BGP13–18, verse frequency

popularity covers most of Central/South America and most of the major countries of Western Europe – in other words largely non-Anglophone nations.

Having pointed to the differences, I also note significant overlaps between the YVP lists and the BGP lists, showing that there is, in fact, a link between extensive engagement (searching, consuming) with the Bible (BGP series), and more intensive engagement with those verses (bookmarking, highlighting and sharing) (YVP series). So, the top three verses (John 3:16, Jeremiah 29:11 and Philippians 4:13) are shared between the two groups of lists, as are Philippians 4:6, Joshua 1:9 and Romans 12:2.

The BGP series of lists include more verses which might be termed 'theocentric' or 'propositional' and which talk explicitly about divine agency – for example, John 3:16, Romans 8:28 and Psalm 23:4. In fact, the two Romans verses are quite instructive in this. Romans 8:28 appears in an almost regular fourth place in the BGP series. The verse states: "And we know that in all things God works for the good of those who love him, who have been called according to his purpose". To some extent the verse is a more theocentric, less future-focussed version of Jeremiah 29:11. Whilst we might critique Jeremiah 29:11 as a hopeful wish that God will sort things out, Romans 8:28 offers an assertion ("We know") that God does work things out "in all things". In the verse Paul proposes that God's plans are tried and tested, and found to be worthy of our trust. The verse is all about direct divine intervention on behalf of those who are part of the believing community. As I will show in the next chapter, this sort of direct divine intervention tends to lie outside the normal parameters of MTD but would fit well into Day's concept of practice-based performative belief.

In contrast, Romans 12:2 calls for an attitudinal shift in our thinking about worldly things: we are not to conform to the pattern of the world. This verse fits into the broad therapeutic category without talking of divine agency at all. Of course, it does mention God's will and as such is not totally anthropocentric. Indeed, Biblical scholars might point to the passive verb in the second clause ('be transformed') as a good example of the divine passive, which tends to be used to highlight divine agency. Regardless of the specialist theological syntax, this verse still feels very 'anthropocentric': we are active agents in our own transformation and it is our judgement and, even, our approval of God's will that matters. As such, Romans 12:2 fits well into the category of therapeutic verses.

3. BGA15, BGA16

Having looked at *BibleGateway*'s series of lists representing extensive engagement (BGP13–18), I now turn to their lists representing much more intensive engagement. In both 2015 and 2016, *BibleGateway* offered a list of verses ranked by the number of times Bible verses that were highlighted or annotated in 2015, or by notes, highlights or favourites in 2016 (BibleGateway, 2015, 2016). The two lists are presented differently. On one hand, in BGA15, one list of ten verses is provided for all annotations. On the other hand, BGA16 is split into three columns of 25 verses, with each column presenting a different mode of social media engagement: annotation, highlighting and favouriting. In order to provide some possibilities for comparison, I developed an aggregate list for BGP16 by taking the ranking position of each verse in each column and adding the three figures together. If a verse was not listed in a column, I added an extra 26 to the score as the original *BibleGateway* list gives 25 answers. This results in an aggregated list for BGA16. In Table 4.3, the aggregate scoring for BGA16 is provided at the end of the Bible verse citation.

When I compare the BPG lists to the BGA lists, I note that John 3:16 almost disappears. It is true that it does maintain a position in the list through an aggregate appearance in BGA16, but in a minor position: 10th most popular annotated verse, 18th most highlighted and 14th most favourited. This is intriguing because in both BGP15 and 16, John 3:16 is the most popular verse on the platform; in BGP 15 (BibleGateway, 2015) is it also noted as being the most popular verse across all the countries which *BibleGateway* singles out: USA, Canada, UK and Australia. The data confirm what I have already found, John 3:16 remains a popular verse in online bible engagement, more popular in extensive engagement (searching, consuming), but much less popular in intensive engagement (annotating, highlighting, favouriting). Later I will compare online engagement specifically with John 3:16, Jeremiah 29:11 and Philippians 4:13.

Similarly, when comparing the BGP and BGA lists, verses from 1 Corinthians 13 and Psalm 23 disappear. It is worth noting that both passages are frequently used in marriages and funerals, which may be one of the few places where the general public now encounters the Bible (Ford et al., 2019). As such, people may well be searching for these texts within those contexts rather than to read this section of the Bible. So, Psalm 23 and 1 Corinthians 13 are just about the most popular chapters in their respective books of the Bible according to *BibleGateway*'s annual popularity grids (for example, BibleGateway, 2015), but the searches are limited to small portions of those texts rather than the whole chapter.

Again, the broad sweep of verses in these lists – which represent more intensive engagement with the text – reflects mostly 'anthropocentric' or 'therapeutic' verses which do not refer directly to divine agency. In fact, it is notable that John 3:16, Proverbs 3:5–6 and even Jeremiah 29:11 – verses which do have direct mention of God/the Lord – appear lower in the BGA16 list than in extensive lists which I have explored so far. Indeed,

Table 4.3 BGP13–18

2015 (BGA15)	2016 (BGA16)	Annotated Verses
1	1	Philippians 4:6: "Do not be anxious about anything, but in every situation, by prayer and petition, with thanksgiving, present your requests to God". (1 + 1 + 1)
2	2	Romans 12:2: "Do not conform to the pattern of this world; but be transformed by the renewing of your mind". (2 + 3 + 4)
3	7	Jeremiah 29:11: "'For I know the plans I have for you', declares the Lord, 'plans to prosper you and not to harm you, plans to give you hope and a future'". (12 + 9 + 3)
4	9	Proverbs 3:5–6: "Trust in the Lord with all your heart and lean not on your own understanding. In all your ways submit to him, and he will make your paths straight". (20 + 8 + 6)
5	8	Philippians 4:8: "Finally, brothers and sisters, whatever is true, whatever is noble, whatever is right, whatever is pure, whatever is lovely, whatever is admirable – if anything is excellent or praiseworthy – think about such things". (16 + 4 + 7)
6	6	Romans 8:28: "And we know that in all things God works for the good of those who love him, who have been called according to his purpose". (11 + 5 + 5)
7	5	Galatians 5:22: "But the fruit of the Spirit is love, joy, peace, forbearance, kindness, goodness, faithfulness". (5 + 7 + 9)
8	4	Ephesians 6:12: "For our struggle is not against flesh and blood, but against the rulers, against the authorities, against the powers of this dark world and against the spiritual forces of evil in the heavenly realms". (3 + 6 + 10)
9		Philippians 4:13: "I can do all this through him who gives me strength". (26 + 13 + 8)
10		Matthew 6:33: "But seek first his kingdom and his righteousness, and all these things will be given to you as well". (24 + 26 + 24)
	3	Philippians 4:7: "And the peace of God, which transcends all understanding, will guard your hearts and your minds in Christ Jesus". (6 + 2 + 2)
	10	John 3:16: "For God so loved the world that he gave his one and only Son, that whoever believes in him shall not perish but have eternal life". (10 + 18 + 14 = 42)

the aggregate score of Jeremiah 29:11 is instructive: it appears 12th in the most annotated verse list, 9th in the highlighted list and 3rd in the favourited list. Annotation of a passage is the most intensive activity (studying, noting, remarking). At the other end, favouriting (or liking) is simply a press of a button on the app/website. So, the third most popular Bible verse in likes is the 12th most annotated. In other words, as the level of engagement increases, the popularity of the verse in the list decreases. Is this because people 'like' the verse but are not really too interested in annotating it or highlighting it? Upon closer inspection does Jeremiah 29:11 lose some of its lustre? Indeed, when we look at the 'top four' Bible verses across different lists, we can see that very few of them are annotated: Philippians 4:13 does not appear in the top 25 verses annotated, but is placed 8th in the list of favourited verses; Romans 8:28 is 12th in the annotation list, but 5th in both the highlighted and favourited lists. Romans 12:2 and Philippians 4:6, however – fundamentally 'anthropocentric'/'therapeutic' verses – are popular in annotating, highlighting *and* favouriting.

It may be that the most popular verses are taken at 'face value' and users do not feel that they need to be annotated or engaged with in the same depth. Nonetheless, users did feel a need to annotate verses which appear close to existing popular verses – such as Romans 12:1 (third in the annotation list in BGA16) and Philippians 4:7 (sixth in that list) – which seems to suggest that popular verses attract attention to their neighbours within the wider context, *contra* the argument about fragmentation that I noted earlier (Siker, 2017; Weaver, 2017b).

But the preponderance of 'therapeutic' or 'experiential' verses over propositional verses is clear. Intensive engagement with the text seems to focus in on such verses. People who are engaging intensively with the text are especially annotating verses which talk of the need for inner renewal or inner therapy rather than texts which focus on creedal doctrines of the Christian Church. Indeed, it is especially notable that the only text from the Gospel in any of the lists studied so far is John 3:16 – and I have shown that this text itself exhibits some interesting underlying trends. The most popular verses do not mention Jesus' life, death or resurrection, nor indeed his teaching. This seems quite a startling revelation when compared to Bible reception outside of social media. Is this a pointer to the predominance of MTD in social media rather than a more general shift (back) towards therapy?

However, in her conversations with young British evangelicals, Ruth Perrin notes that she did not find clear evidence of MTD (Perrin, 2016, pp. 144, 172, 226) but rather her interviewees talked in terms of orthodox, propositional truth. This is interesting because it maps back to Day's discussion of performative belief in which interviewees responded in surveys with orthodoxy but their practice suggested something else. Is it the case that in interviews, in interactional engagement with another person, people present themselves in presumed agreement with their interviewer (a form of confirmation bias), but in unobserved engagement online, they present a different type of performance? This suggests that there might be a mismatch not only between surveys and 'real life', but also between ethnographic interviews and "ordinary social performance of bible engagement on social media" (Smith and Denton, 2005, pp. 67–71; see also Perrin, 2016). This might suggest that that difference is something linked to the affordances of social media itself. Perhaps this is part of the wider media ecology?

4. Lists representing active social sharing (YVS14–15, OB14–15, OBRT15)

YouVersion provided lists of verses actively shared on social media in both 2014 and 2015 (YouVersion, 2014, 2015). In addition, *OpenBible* provides lists of Bible verses shared on Twitter in both 2014 and 2015 (Smith, 2014, 2015) and also a list of the most popular Bible verses retweeted (by celebrities) on Twitter in 2015 (Smith, 2015).

Sharing verses is the most intensive type of online social performance. It represents a quasi-public performance of faith, a statement of identity visible to the sharer's online community and potentially to the general public (dependent on security settings). As such, I would expect these lists to incorporate verses with which the social media users strongly identify, enough to want to broadcast this to their respective online communities and, with Twitter, potentially complete strangers and the general public.

The problem is how to bring these lists together into a composite table as developed in the previous groups of lists. In the end, the process became far too convoluted with the five lists covering 44 verses in total with just under half (19) appearing on only one list each. Across the two YVS lists, of the ten verses on YVS14, none appear on YVS15, whilst 50% of the verses on OB14 appear on OB15 (Philippians 4:13; Proverbs 3:5; 2 Timothy 1:7; Psalm 56:3, 1 Peter 5:7), of these only Proverbs 3:5 appears on any another of these lists (YVS15). Only one verse (Jeremiah 29:11) of those retweeted by celebrities appears on any of the other lists. (The lists are all given in Chapter 3.) It is perhaps better not to attempt a tabulation since there are no clear trends in verse selection to be picked up across such a diverse set of Bible verses. However, there are some interesting points to be made.

In the YVS lists, five out of nine verses in YVS14 are drawn from the Hebrew Bible, but only one appears in any other list (2 Chronicles 7:14 appears also in KJV12). There no verses common to both YVS14 and YVS15. Overall, the verses in YVS14 exhibit little resemblance to other *YouVersion* lists. As it stands, YVS14 seems to stand out and may well be a rogue list. Having said that, the Hebrew Bible verses shared in this list represent reminders of God's action or abiding presence (1 Chronicles 16:34, Psalm 103:17–18, Joshua 1:9) and/or a challenge to respond to God's love in some way (2 Chronicles 7:14, Jeremiah 33:2–3, Deuteronomy 6:6–7, Proverbs 3:5–6). What is clear that these are 'theocentric' verses: the centre of focus of activity and agency is in God. In contrast, YVS15 contains a number of popular tweets across all 20 lists: Proverbs 3:5, Philippians 4:6, Joshua 1:9 and Romans 12:2, all of which I have previously noted tend to reflect 'therapeutic' values, as does Romans 15:13, a verse unique to this list.

As I showed in Chapter 2, sharing a Bible verse creates an interactional performance between the social media user and their audience: 'this is the God in whom I believe'. Moreover, it is an invitation to the audience to add their own assent to this understanding of God. If I am right in my earlier analysis of the texts, then in YVS14 users offered an interactional performance based on mostly 'theocentric' texts. However, in YVS15, users shifted their interactional performance to mostly therapeutic texts. This shift from 'propositional' to 'therapeutic' has already been noted; it is made all the more obvious in the gradually improving performance of Jeremiah 29:11. The transition matches both an increasingly MTD or 'practice-led belief' model and an increasingly therapeutic media ecology. Both would create increasing pressure for Bible sharers to play the social media game and to perform the Bible in a manner acceptable to the preconditions and preferences of social media – that is, to refrain from overt messages about God's activity and to focus much more on hopeful verses, therapeutic verses and happy verses which are much more likely to be retweeted and liked.

The same process can be seen in the *OpenBible* lists: a preference for therapeutic verses. It is important to note that one of the most 'therapeutic' verses, Philippians 4:13, is tweeted more than twice any other verse in OB14 – but actually the combined number of tweets across both lists drops by almost 50% between OB14 (2.53 million) and OB15 (1.31 million). It seems that by 2015 many fewer verses were being shared on Twitter. Were people less keen to perform their Bible engagement on the platform because Twitter had become a much less receptive place to Tweet about the Bible than it had been in 2014?

OBRT15 is a unique list in that it also gives us a glimpse of the Bible within celebrity culture – a glimpse of celebrity social performance of Bible engagement within digital culture (Phillips, 2019). The tweets originate from and reflect aspects of an interesting mix of different cultures. They are visual artefacts that appear in Twitter's livestreams as brief text messages always accompanied by the avatar representing the celebrity who has issued the tweet and sometimes with additional images appended to the tweet.

It is important to note the different elements of these tweets, both textual and visual. Demi Lovato's tweet in sixth position includes only her avatar and the text "Jeremiah 29:11" and Cameron Dallas's tweet in fourth position includes his avatar and the text "Romans 8:18" accompanied by a smiling (flushed?) face emoji. In these tweets, the textual baggage of the tweet is minimal. It is perhaps assumed that the reader will know the text cited through their own devotional engagement with the Bible. This may well point to the celebrity tweeter's own devotional engagement as well.

Some tweets contain a paraphrase of the text. So, Dallas's other retweet in the list, referencing Psalm 16:11, contains a specific (and rare) translation of the verse. It is probable that this version of the verse arises from prosperity/holiness spirituality, but the source is unknown. The paraphrase enables a specific emphasis to be placed on the tweet which may well appeal to the tweeter or to the assumed cultural paradigms of the expected audience.

The second and seventh largest retweets (1 Corinthians 13:13 and John 1:5) were both sent from Ally Brooke Hernandez's account. Both tweets include the text of the Bible verse and the citation. The tweet citing 1 Corinthians 13 also includes a heart emoji. Manny Pacquiao, a boxer well known for his political and social activism in the Philippines, tweets Psalm 120:1 in a similar format of Bible verse (reference and text, including capitalization of the divine name). Again, Timothy Tebow, an American football athlete renowned for being disciplined after painting John 3:16 on his face before a football match, cites Ephesians 4:32 with the full text of the Bible verse. These last three celebrity tweeters – Brooke, Pacquiao and Tebow – provide normally unaccompanied verses in a style very close to or identical to that of verses shared from the major Bible websites and mobile applications. It is almost as if these verses are highlighted in and shared from a Bible app. The emphasis is much more on the text in these instances, as emphasized by the use of quotation marks. The only visual elements are the avatar and the use of the heart emoji in one of the tweets.

Siwon Choi, a devout Korean Christian and boyband member/movie star, tweets a reference to a whole Bible chapter – 'Colossians 3' – and accompanies this with a picture of himself riding a police motorcycle. The connection with Colossians 3 seems tenuous. Perhaps it is a reference to new clothes? The dominance and impact of the picture seems to be the invitation for retweeting here rather than the ambiguous Bible reference. Indeed, one might ask why the Bible reference is included at all, since it seems to bear little weight in this context. The Bible verse may well be being used as an evangelistic hook, seeking to encourage Choi's fans to read the larger text.

The top retweet (Philippians 1:3) was originally tweeted from the account of Maine Mendoza, a Philippine actress who is best known for her viral Dubsmash video and is now a successful television personality. Mendoza has 3.3 million followers on Twitter. The (now deleted) tweet puts together a reference to Philippians 1:3 (no text) with a picture of Mendoza with fellow actor Alden Richards and the rather cryptic hashtag #ALDUB5th-Monthsary. The hashtag and picture refer to the hugely popular onscreen relationship between Mendoza and Richards ("Aldub"). If we therefore put together the different aspects of this tweet, we begin to see why it is so popular – a popular celebrity, playing a popular character, celebrating love, by using a Bible verse in a deeply Biblical culture. However, the lack of a direct quotation undermines the Bible reference because it makes a vague reference to a text which is assumed to be known by its intended audience. My instinct is that people were retweeting the picture and its hashtag, and that the verse reference came along with it as a passenger, much like the previous tweet from Siwon Choi.

All of these tweets seem to reflect aspects of the personal faith response of celebrities to various contexts within societies favourably disposed towards the Bible. The number of retweets seems to be linked not to the specific Bible verses but to an image associated with the tweet, even if it is only the avatar of the celebrity. Sometimes, especially with those celebrities seemingly tweeting from within Bible apps, the text takes precedent. However, in others, not least in the last two (which are accompanied by pictures), the Bible text seems to be a passive component or a passenger within a predominantly visual culture. The visual content in these dominates over the text and the texts ride undercover, perhaps cultural hints or markers.

5. Intensive lists and social performance

I have noted that sharing Bible verses on social media operates as an interactional performance of Bible engagement: 'this is the God in whom I believe'. Moreover, it is an invitation to the audience to add its assent to this understanding of God. I also noted that the number of tweets of Bible verses decreased between 2014 and 2015 and switched from being mostly 'theocentric' to mostly 'therapeutic'. As such, there seems to be some pressure to conform to social media 'rules' which may well have affected this change. In the next chapter, I will look at how media ecology may well have affected this switch. But there is also the possibility that the act of sharing also acts as an invitation for the recipient of a Tweet/share to empathize with the sharer and assent to the understanding of God in that text. In an important way, this shifts a 'therapeutic'/'anthropocentric' text into a 'propositional'/'theocentric' text: the performance of therapy offers a proposition about faith as therapeutic and about God as a healer. In YVS14, I would then note the propositions about God through pretty standard 'theocentric' texts. However, I would then need to see YVS15 as offering a characterization of God which was much more in line with the God proposed in MTD or in practice-led belief rather than through traditional expressions of Christian theology.

Let's take, for example, the use of Philippians 4:8 (YVS14 and three other lists among the total 20 being studied): "Finally, brothers and sisters, whatever is true, whatever is noble, whatever is right, whatever is pure, whatever is lovely, whatever is admirable – if anything is excellent or praiseworthy – think about such things". This verse provides a moral focus for readers of the Bible, both direct and practical (as long as you understand the terms). It promotes an ethical approach to (media) consumption which fits well within contemporary culture. Moreover, its relative ambiguity leaves the individual reader to define what exactly fits into the acceptable moral categories. It is notable, for example, that the lists of specific virtues and vices found in Galatians 5:19–24 do not appear in any of the lists. Instead, Philippians 4:8 can be read in a way that suggests that as long as an individual maintains their own ethical standards in their visual, conceptual and actual consumption of contemporary culture, they will receive peace from God.

But it is notable that this verse is taken out of the context of the wider Philippian letter which is founded on some distinctly Christological propositions (Philippians 2, for example). For Paul, an encounter with Christ – through his incarnation, life, work, death, resurrection and ascension – is essential to the overall argument which he constructs in the letter. But this verse is taken out of that context and shared on its own without comment or commentary. Like most of the shared verses in YVS14 and YVS15, there is no mention of any direct intervention from God (or Jesus). Individuals are responsible for their behaviour, their consumption and their lifestyle. God has already established the reward received by those who act in this way – the presence of the God of peace, the inheritance they are due – the 'Divine Butler' smiling encouragingly from the side of the room.

Interestingly, Galatians 6:7–8 (shared in YVS14), perhaps the least MTD-focussed verse to be shared, in fact follows exactly the same pattern. On the one hand, this looks different from those other 'therapeutic' verses: it is true that there is here a slightly different understanding of God from the usual MTD 'Divine Butler' image. There is a sense that the creator has made all things in a specific way, with a specific purpose; that there is a divinely initiated way to live out one's life, and that by failing to recognize this, we seek to mock that creator. The verse seems to suggest that resistance to God's ways (sowing to please the flesh) will lead to corruption, but acceptance of God's ways (sowing to please the Spirit) will lead to eternal life. This is not quite direct intervention from God. There is still here a sense that proper therapeutic behaviour will bring therapeutic awards. Interestingly, in Jeremiah 33:2–3 (also in the list) we are told that God – who made the earth, formed it and established it – vocalizes his presence. But instead of the resulting polarity in outcomes, God seems to offer himself as a form of divine search engine: "Call to me and I will answer you and tell you great and unsearchable things you do not know". God's call seems to take us back once again to MTD.

I've already argued that sharing verses on social media offers an interactional performance declaring the beliefs of the sharer, of the individual. It is a way in which the sharer states the kind of beliefs with which they wish to be associated and which they are happy to share with their online communities. Some of those verses argue that the life of faith has potential to change the reader – that the life of faith and its God have aspects of agency attached to them. God is not just a 'Divine Butler', and we are not the only ones who have control. So, we might look at Colossians 3:24, shared in YVS14: "since you know that you will receive an inheritance from the Lord as a reward. It is the Lord Christ you are serving". This is not totally about an individualized inheritance. The end of that verse recognizes that working hard identifies the *YouVersion* reader/sharer as a servant of Christ. So also, Galatians 6:7–8 and Jeremiah 33:2–3 point to the role of God in directing the performance of faith in the life of the believer. In the end, these verses promote an active change to belief initiated by the presence (and activity?) of the divine. God has established the world in a specific way and faith performance demands awareness to this – and perhaps conformity to it.

Sharing such verses online as an act of interactional performative belief creates an interestingly different identity marker to that which we have seen elsewhere. It merges together therapeutic texts with propositional assertions about divine activity/agency and the life of the believer. Those sharing these verses seem to be signalling to their online communities that there is more to this faith that is being shared than mere individualism.

Indeed, the texts themselves become an enactment of the performative belief which they themselves promote. So, Deuteronomy 6:6–7 (shared in YVS14) begins with an internalization of the commands given in the previous verses, the iconic *Shema* prayer, one of the defining markers of Jewish identity. But then the second of the verses calls for direct action to install this teaching into the lifeblood of both individual and community: the words are to be taught diligently to the children, to be talked about in social and private discourse, and at all times. Indeed, the sharing of these verses by *YouVersion* users would seem to be an obedient direct enactment of the command of God to communicate this message at all times by all means. By sharing these verses, the users are actually obeying God's command by sharing core aspects of their faith online (Cheong, 2012). This is not the individualistic agency of therapeutic moralism, but rather a performative, observed marking of one's identity, a public display of otherness, within social media sharing: 'this is who I am'.

Performative belief

So, a number of verses in these lists reflect the direct communication of – and hence performative identification with – a God of both numinous and powerful presence. There is a potential switch here in the online performance of the social media user which makes therapeutic texts into propositional, performative belief. So, when discussing Day's concept of performative belief, James Beckford proposed looking at performative belief through a different form of analysis which focussed on "the speaker's strategies for displaying their competence as rational 'doers' of believing in particular social settings". He then proposes: "'Doing believing' would involve the rhetorical, linguistic, and semantic 'moves' that speakers routinely make in order to 'bring off' a performance of belief" (Beckford in Cotter, 2016, pp. 102–103). What I see here in my analysis of performative belief on social media is the decision by those who share Bible verses on social media to share verses which promote more 'propositional' verses or to make 'therapeutic' verses into 'propositional' by their own performance of them. Indeed, it is never an either/or discussion. As Day notes, she is proposing "a wider typology of belief, showing the interrelationship among propositional, felt (emotional-embodied), and performative modes" (Day in Cotter, 2016, p. 113).

More broadly, what seems to be happening is that when people are not observed, their performance aligns with MTD or experiential Christianity; but when people are more active in their social sharing, when they are performing their belief, they tend to reflect a more propositional position in which faith and the divine have potential agency in the life of both the sharer and the recipient. Whilst Day's interviews led to a feeling of disjunction between formal religion and performative belief, in the online context, intensive performative belief (here signified by sharing texts) seems to push people back towards a more formal religion/'propositional' engagement with the Bible, which they tend not to exhibit in their (unobserved) extensive performance (searching, consuming).

Remember that *YouVersion*'s data covers all aspects of society, not just those who reflect the values of MTD. As such the verses shared and the sentiments behind that sharing will reflect many different contemporary expressions of faith, some of which may well include elements of propositional and therapeutic Christianity. Moreover, we have seen that Christian Smith's own discussion of MTD suggested that when people were challenged about faith, they tended to revert to more conservative, propositional elements of Christian understanding (Smith and Denton, 2005, pp. 67–71; Perrin, 2016). In the difference between these two pairs of data sets (YVP14/YVP15 and YVS14/YVS15), we have potentially found a good example of how that difference works. The therapeutic focus of MTD is demonstrated

86 *Analysis/reflection*

through (non-observed, operant) bookmarking and highlighting, almost entirely resulting in popular verses which talk much more of therapy than of propositions or interventions. However, when we move to verses which are shared, which seem to display something of identity (thus observed, espoused), we find that users are keen to identify with some central markers of traditional faith communities and to recognize much more the role of the divine in the establishment of ethical living and on the reward associated with living that life out. This matches Smith's suggestion that those influenced by MTD have a dual identity: internally, they follow the basic practices of MTD-type Christianity, but outwardly they connect with more traditional forms of Christianity and Christian practice.

Google Trends

Of course, what I am not saying here is that Bible verses such as John 3:16 – verses which specifically mention Jesus or specifically point to an interventionist God, what I have referred to through this analysis as 'theocentric' or 'propositional verses – are not found on the internet. They are, in abundance. So, for example, a search on Google for John 3:16 returns a massive 94.1 million results, whereas Jeremiah 29:11 returns 6.1 million results. This research is about the ordinary social performance of Bible engagement in digital culture, and I have spent this chapter analyzing 20 lists of popular Bible verse lists which provide the core data for my research. A Google search simply shows how often that verse is present on the internet. I would expect John 3:16 to be very well represented in pre-digital texts on the web. But, for my purposes, it is much more important to look at how these verses are used in contemporary online experience.

As defined by Google, Google Trends is a public web facility, based on Google Search, that shows how often a particular search term is entered relative to the total search volume across various regions of the world, and in various languages. As such, it finds extensive engagement. In this exercise I typed in three search strings: for Jeremiah 29:11, one for John 3:16 and one for Philippians 4:13 (yellow).[2]

The resulting diagram, shown in Figure 4.2, reveals that Jeremiah 29:11 is, first of all, a more popular search term than John 3:16. Second, I note the regular patterning of John 3:16 around two events: March 16 (John 3:16 Day) and Easter in the Western Church traditions. I can determine the dates of Easter precisely by those peaks. Interestingly, the highest peaks for John 3:16 are mirrored by falling usage of Jeremiah 29.11, which is much more erratic and unstable. The heartbeat pattern of John 3.16 seems to reflect an increasingly liturgical use of the verse around major Christian festivals, an institutionalization of the search term. Moreover, the term is diminishing

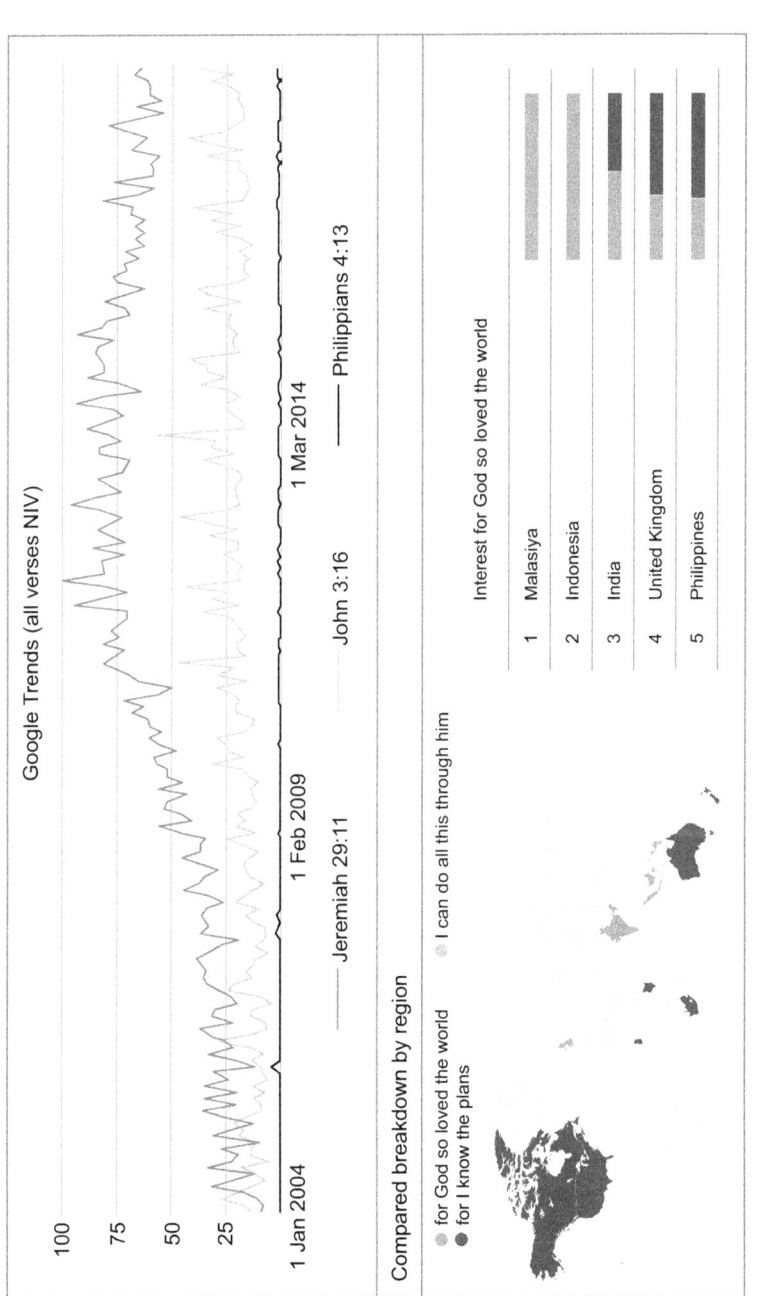

Figure 4.2 Google Trends, NIV translations for Jeremiah 29:11, John 3:16, Philippians 4:13

gradually, although so is the frequency of Jeremiah 29:11 from 2015. Interestingly, Philippians 4:13 is not on the radar at all as a search term. Having said that, the results could be read in a different way: the 'theocentric' John 3:16 remains stable; the new challenger, 'therapeutic" Jeremiah 29:11, is erratic and in decline: and if you put Philippians 4:13 into the algorithm in its King James Version (KJV) format ("I can do all things through Christ"), then it actually supersedes both of the others (Figure 4.3). Although this new version shows the power of the KVJ and its role within the evangelical wing of the Church and the difference is replacing "in him" with "in Christ", which is not in the original Greek. The verse does intend "him" to be read as "Christ", but technically the title is not used in the original. Even so, the trend remains, with both 'therapeutic' verses showing vibrant engagement (although declining since 2015), while John 3:16 remains within its institutionalized stability. Google Trends suggests that the lists are perhaps a little more conservative than I expected: 'therapeutic' verses are almost 50% more popular as search terms than the classic 'theocentric' verse.

Conclusion

Analysis of the 20 lists which form my data set for the ordinary social performance of Biblical engagement in digital culture shows that on the whole there is a trend towards engaging with 'therapeutic' or 'anthropocentric' Bible verses in online engagement. Although I have noted the use of more 'propositional texts' on the *BibleGateway* platform and in lists which relate to more intensive engagement, particularly public sharing, even here the tendency to make use of 'therapeutic' verses stands out.

What are the implications of this analysis? In Chapter 5, I will note the similarity between my findings and those in Day's work on performative belief and Christian Smith's work on MTD. Both have argued for a shift from 'propositional/theocentric' expressions of belief to 'therapeutic/anthropocentric' expressions. I will explore this in some depth.

This does mean that at present there remains a balance between 'therapeutic' and 'propositional' verses. It is not true to say that everything has become 'therapeutic'; moreover, the Google Trends graph showing a decline in 'therapeutic' verses in web searching suggests that ongoing research is needed to see whether what I am seeing here is an historic pattern rather than a future pattern. Moreover, different parts of the world, different cultures and different sections of society will respond in different ways. Further research is needed to continue to explore the data which both *BibleGateway* and *YouVersion* hold about Bible engagement in today's digital world.

This also means that the Bible 'seen' on social media tends to be a 'therapeutic' text rather than a 'propositional' text. Whereas art through the ages

Figure 4.3 Google Trends, Jeremiah 29:11 (NIV), John 3:16 (NIV), Philippians 4:13 (KJV)

has tended to focus on representing the Christian faith in the Gospel message around the life of Christ, in the people associated with that story, as well as through its main events, contemporary social media retells the Christian faith as a faith of self-determination, courage and hope grounded on the belief in 'the Lord' – a rather absent-present divine figure sometimes referred to by other names such as 'Christ'. This 'therapeutic' expression of faith can be seen even in quite 'propositional' verses, especially when they are shared online. Of course, this research does not mean to suggest that either 'therapeutic' or 'propositional' expressions of faith are right or wrong. It simply shows that at this time, in this medium, an increasing number of online expressions of Bible engagement tend to be 'therapeutic' in substance.

Notes

1 The search was undertaken using a VPN set with the perceived location as Toronto and using Google Incognito in order to minimize the localisation and personalisation settings of the search engine.
2 The exercise was carried out on February 26, 2019 and should be retrievable at https://g.co/trends/8Mq4i.

5 Some potential contributory factors
Performative belief, MTD and media ecology

Throughout the conversation so far, I have talked about a conceptual or sociological or practice-based shift around faith expression evidenced in ordinary social media performance of Bible engagement within digital culture. The increase in therapeutic texts seen across the series of lists is symbolically represented in Jeremiah 29:11 'overtaking' John 3:16, but more fundamentally represented in the ongoing trends around both verses, as seen in the Google Trends discussion in the last chapter. John 3:16 is a totemic text (like the Bible in American society) but a text which seems to have settled into an institutionalized pattern of engagement and, in recent lists (YVP17, YVP18), popular only in a limited number of countries where Christianity is in the minority. In contrast, Jeremiah 29:11 is a text which is increasingly popular across multiple cultures, for which there is evidence of increasing popularity on social platforms (though perhaps not on Google Trends) and which is embraced within the broader ecology of a mediated Bible.

Of course, that apparent shift to 'therapeutic' from 'propositional' is quite a complex thing. In the conclusion to Chapter 4, I noted that online social performance of 'therapeutic' texts tended to make such texts operate as 'propositional' texts, since they reflected the belief performance of the social media user: 'therapy' becomes part of the 'propositional' make up of online faith expression. So, when I explored a range of 'therapeutic' texts in light of this finding, these texts became 'propositional' by bringing together aspects of divine agency/presence and 'therapeutic' wellbeing, and thus pointing towards an assertion of identity and challenge to the reader to accept this identity for themselves. I noted both James Beckford's comments on the need to analyze performative belief with new tools to reveal the performer's strategies to 'bring off' a social performance of belief (Beckford in Cotter, 2016, pp. 102–103) and Abby Day's assertion in *Believing in Belonging* that she too was interested in "the wider typology of belief, showing the interrelationship among propositional, felt (emotional-embodied), and performative modes" (Day in Cotter, 2016, p. 113).

92 *Some potential contributory factors*

The aggregate list presented in Chapter 3, Table 3.3, and then explored in various Tables and their analysis in Chapter 4 shows a gradual shift over time from broadly propositional texts to broadly therapeutic texts. Indeed, the shift from popular verses in printed texts to popular verses in social media shows that shift even more clearly. But it remains unclear how much that shift is due to a change in media ecologies (from print to social media) or to a sociological shift proposed by a number of (near) contemporary theologians and sociologists, especially, as previously noted, George Lindbeck's concept of a shift from propositional to experiential expressions of faith (Lindbeck, 2002, pp. 169–195); Grace Davie's shift from formal theology to informal spirituality (Davie, 2000, pp. 176–194); or Stephen Heelas and Linda Woodhead's 'spiritual turn' (Heelas and Woodhead, 2005). A number of ethnographers of youth culture have noted a similar shift among young people towards a more therapeutic focus on life known in the USA as 'moralistic therapeutic deism' (MTD) (Smith and Denton, 2005, pp. 12–13), or, in the UK and Australasia, as the happy midi-narrative (HmN) (Mason, Singleton and Webber, 2005; Collins-Mayo and Beaudoin, 2010; Collins-Mayo et al., 2010; Cusack, 2011; Hughes, 2013a, 2013b). Both construals argue that young people are attracted more to a therapeutic approach to religion than to a propositional approach.

When I am looking at contemporary social performance of Bible engagement, I seem to be tracing a symptom of a much larger religious shift. However, that shift may be evidence that these religious trends are being enhanced or magnified by contemporary media ecology, as argued by Stig Hjarvard, Esther McIntosh and Timothy Hutchings (Hjarvard, 2011, 2013; Hutchings, 2014, 2015, 2017; McIntosh, 2015), amongst others. In this chapter, then, I will provide an overview of MTD; look at various conversations about the spirituality/spiritual expression of young people in contemporary Anglophone society in the West/Global North, noting briefly that the outcomes of this exploration probably also apply to the parents of those millennials; and explore the potential links to changes associated with contemporary media ecology.

Moralistic therapeutic deism

In 2005, Christian Smith, lead researcher on the American *National Study of Youth and Religion*, coined the term MTD to categorize the set of beliefs held by contemporary teens in the USA (Smith and Denton, 2005). MTD, Smith argues, is a distinct version (or 'performance') of Christianity, a set of beliefs based around a perceived need to perform morally, to be engaged in self-improvement and healthy living, and "to do one's best to be successful" (Smith and Denton, 2005, pp. 162–163). He sees MTD not as a new religious movement, but as a set of ideas that seems to be colonizing

Some potential contributory factors 93

mainstream religions across different age groups. Indeed, since Smith argues most teens adopt the belief systems of their parents/guardians, then MTD is as prevalent among American adults as among American teens (Smith and Denton, 2005, pp. 164, 166).

Smith proposes that an MTD creed would sound "something like this":

1   A God exists who created and orders the world and watches over human life on earth
2   God wants people to be good, nice and fair to each other, as taught in the Bible and by most world religions
3   The central goal of life is to be happy and to feel good about oneself
4   God does not need to be particularly involved in one's life except when God is needed to resolve a problem
5   Good people go to heaven when they die

MTD involves belief in a (rather unobtrusive) metaphysical divine being, but it focuses less on the metaphysical aspects of faith and much more on the mundane, on personal wellbeing and interpersonal relationships – in other words it is much closer to the kind of social performance outlined by Day (Day, 2010). So, Smith sums up the central moral focus of MTD as a conviction that you should avoid being socially disruptive or interpersonally obnoxious. MTD sets up a moral code upon its adherents that is applicable across all faiths, but one which is extraordinarily limited in practical detail: as summarized by one Hindu teen interviewed by Smith: "Just don't be an asshole, that's all" (Smith and Denton, 2005, p. 163).

It is likely that the shift from 'propositional' to 'therapeutic' verses is simply one symptom of a much larger phenomenon in 'belief' per se, and also that MTD is but one signal of that shift, not least since other scholars have failed to find evidence for MTD in similar contexts (Perrin, 2016, p. 144, p. 172). This larger shift has been discussed throughout this book from the Introduction onwards; I have made much of the language Day uses about 'anthropocentric' or 'theocentric' performances of belief (Day, 2011, pp. 156–158). Day's work is both inspired by and developed out of the work of Heelas and Woodhead in exploring the disparity between high numbers of people saying that they were Christian but not attending church (Day, 2011, p. 28; Heelas and Woodhead, 2005). Indeed, in the Introduction, I stated that this book is an attempted outworking of Day's construct of performative belief (Day, 2010, p. 26) and an acceptance of Mia Lövheim's challenge to see how that construct plays out in contemporary social media (Lövheim in Cotter, pp. 106–8)

The proposed shift could be mapped against wider sociological and philosophical changes with the so-called decline/demise of metanarratives and the potential relativism of postmodernism. In turn, that social shift matches the economic shift out of post-war austerity into full-blown capitalism and consumerism and the rise of personal computing and the digital age. We are clearly in a time of transglobal cultural shifts. Such changes to our cultures are bound to have an effect on religious expression, which is intimately associated with cultural expression. In his 'Post-Coda' to *The American Religion*, Harold Bloom summarized American millennial religion in these terms: "Be rich, demand love from God and from humans, and have faith that death is only for others". (Bloom, 2006, p. xiii, p. 304). Moreover, researchers have found similar changes in both British and Australasian society (Collins-Mayo and Beaudoin, 2010). In one project, Sylvia Collins-Mayo's team found a similar interpersonally focused faith practiced among the UK's Generation Y: a faith lived out amongst "the 'secular trinity' of family, friends and the reflexive self" (Collins-Mayo et al., 2010, p. 32, p. 50). In a string of articles and book chapters analyzing religion and Generation Z in Australia, Carole Cusack and Philip Hughes, among others, broadly agree on Generation Z's focus on therapeutic wellbeing or even more simply that the "focus of life for almost all young people is on enjoyment" (Cusack, 2011, p. 412; Mason et al., 2005; Hughes 2013a, 2013b).

The replacement of a rigorous dogma and/or metaphysics with a rather less focused, more generalized, therapeutic vocabulary is the key aspect of MTD/HmN. But it is also the key focus of Day's performative belief – an expression of believing which is less focused on the propositions of faith than on a practice-based faith, and a faith based on how it is lived out in practice rather than on the doctrines it seeks to maintain. The focus is not on what I must believe or in whom I must believe, but rather how I live my life (Day, 2010, p. 11; Bloom, 2006, p. 17, p. 32). Whilst traditional, doctrinal Christianity might understand Christian healing/therapy in metaphysical terms of redemption, salvation and a cure for original sin, MTD offers the chance for an immediate personalized therapy, of feeling good about yourself in the here and now. In different religious traditions, interviewees spoke of their assurance that religious practice "makes me feel better about myself", "It's relaxing. It's sort of like therapeutic" – a recreation of religion into an immediately accessible therapeutic commodity (Smith and Denton, 2005, p. 164; Mason et al., 2005, p. 19).

Such shifts, moreover, are not limited to the latest generations. Day's embedded ethnographical research in North Yorkshire followed women across three generations, all of whom practice some form of performative belief. Smith and Denton's study argues strongly that most American teenagers are actually quite conservative in their adoption of traditional religious patterns and communities, and they overtly reject the popular concept of a postmodern pick and mix 'religion free' spirituality, saying that it is not present in the survey's findings, and strongly criticize the body of literature "promot[ing] the alleged dramatic religious pluralism of the contemporary United States", "empirically that idea is simply an overblown and erroneous claim" (Smith and Denton, 2005, p. 261). A Pew Research report by Paul Taylor in the USA (Taylor, 2017), and Ingrid Storm and David Voas's work on intergenerational faith transmission (Storm and Voas, 2012,) seem to support Smith and Denton's argument that the shift in religious expression is gradual over generations: parents are likely to believe in MTD almost as much as their children.

After noting that MTD is primarily engaged in morality rather than metaphysics, Smith noted that his interviewees pictured God as a rather passive and inactive benevolent force: a producer; a monitor who stands in the wings watching what is happening, waiting to intervene when needed; "selectively available for taking care of [people's] needs" (Smith and Denton, 2005, p. 165). Theologically, this is why Smith adopts the classic 18th century term 'deism' because of its lack of metaphysical engagement with the Biblical tradition. God seems more to be 'a god' than the Biblical Yahweh/Jesus. Smith's key images of God from MTD are Divine Clockmaker establishing both creation and the laws that govern creation; Divine Butler waiting in the shadows to come to the assistance of those who believe in him; and Cosmic Therapist ensuring that his clients feel good and socially successful. Smith notes that one of the key aspects of such a God is that, in the words of a 17-year-old conservative Protestant girl from Florida, "He doesn't talk back". In other words, this God is there to serve our needs, without putting demands upon us - perhaps as a projection of a perfect, non-demanding, all-providing parent. At the same time, Robert Wuthnow's exploration of contemporary American religion took a similar tack: "Sacredness ceases to be the *mysterium tremendum* that commands awe and reverence and becomes a house pet that does our bidding" (Wuthnow, 1994, p. 255). Less pejoratively, in their study of Australian youth, Michael Mason et al. (2005, p. 18) wonder whether their interviewee's spirituality reflects apophatic Eastern Christianity:

I: *So what do you think God is like?*
S: I've never imagined what God would be like or what he looks like but he's just God.
I: *So what do you believe about God?*
S: God, he did a lot for us. I mean, he's God. I get funny sort of talking about him. I don't know what to say.

Smith realizes that there are limitations to his concept of MTD. He argues that MTD acts as a parasite living off a host religion, or as a virus inserting itself into the nucleus of the host and seeking to make changes. So, MTD modifies the host religion, minimizing the metaphysical, structural, doctrinal aspects of that religion and emphasizing a new therapeutic core of both belief and practice. Many aspects of the host religion, both in terms of belief and practice, will be maintained within such a process, as Smith found. But the centre of causation within the religion will have changed from the metaphysical to the human. Doctrine will be less important; self-improvement will be everything. So, when interviewers talked to teens about their religious experience, teens answered not in traditional doctrinal phrases (sin, redemption, salvation, Bible, holiness, loving one's neighbour) but in the language of therapy (personally feeling, being made happy, feeling good about life, feeling better, satisfied, fulfilled). "Feeling happy" appears over 2,000 times in the transcripts of interviews taken (Smith and Denton, 2005, p. 168; Collins-Mayo and Beaudoin, 2010, p. 17).

But is this form of 'practice-based faith' such a novelty? Is there a pristine form of 'propositional' Christianity which MTD is transforming? Smith and Denton's work may well be in danger of suggesting that post-Reformation forms of Christianity, especially those based on Enlightenment rationality and American Evangelicalism, have always been the norm, when we know that Christianity has historically had many forms and many traditions. I showed in Chapter 2 that 'civic religion' in the USA (Gorski, 2010) did not maintain close adherence to the words of the Bible but focused on more general Biblical images associating the pioneers with early Israel. Indeed, many aspects of both civic religion and Christian nationalism might be seen to be forms of practice-based religion. Moreover, 'religion as therapy' is hardly a new concept in the study of religion. At the end of the first century, John's Gospel states that Jesus came in order that humanity might have life in all its fullness (John 10:10) and goes on to argue that true discipleship is revealed through the disciples' love for one other (John 13:35). Ignatius of Antioch, in his Letter to the Ephesians (verse 14) referred to Christian faith and practice as "the cure of sick souls" and "the medicine of immortality"; in his Letter to the Romans (verse 20) referred to Christian ministers as *therapeutes*. That was taken up literally within the monastic tradition; the association between health care and the Christian Church remains central in many global societies. Some might argue that MTD follows in this same therapeutic tradition. If we are thriving in terms of our personal and social wellbeing, then are we not living out the very essence of the shalom of God? Is this not the lived faith, the espoused faith of practical theology, the ordinary theology of Jeff Astley and others?

Smith's discovery of adolescents embracing what Linda Woodhead calls the "spiritual turn" or the shift towards the subjective (Woodhead, 2007), or Abby Day refers to as 'practice-based faith', in their articulation of faith is not particularly surprising, given both the contemporary context and the nature of adolescent faith identity (Bachand, 2010; Day, 2011, pp. 74–98). What is more notable here is that there is an acceptance of partial continuity between generations. MTD may be as much a religious phenomenon among adults as among young people. But again, this might be a phenomenon of wider societal shifts which cross generations and cultures. I note, for example, postmodernism's rejection of objectivity in preference to radical subjectivity and the shift towards less authoritarian models of faith (Ward, 1997, pp. xv–xliii). Perhaps Smith's MTD therefore should be seen as a part of a trans-religious, trans-geographic and trans-generational shift (back) towards a more 'practice-based belief' – a 'believing in belonging'.

Another major criticism of Smith's research is his assumption that his interviewees were in fact incapable of articulating a fully formed (adult?) theological narrative – that their contribution was a partial articulation of their faith. Sarah Caffrey Bachand has argued that although MTD does represent "the presence of an inadequate and to some degree inauthentic faith", it does so because it represents "a 21st-century American version of an *adolescent* faith". (Bachand, 2010, p. 143). In other words, with all that we know about religious development and faith education, would we expect anything much more sophisticated? Indeed, drawing on developmental theory, Bachand argues that the subjective nature of adolescent faith (as opposed to the objectification of adult faith) means that teen faith is "a tacit faith that cannot be reflected on, handled, and so on, in the same way that adult faith can be" (Bachand, 2010, p. 149).

This is not the only criticism which Bachand levels at Smith's construct. Along with her argument that adolescents should not be expected to articulate faith in an objective manner, Bachand also makes the point that the God represented in MTD reflects a *traditional* understanding of God found throughout Judaeo-Christian traditions and texts – that of a therapeutic God. God *is* there. God *does* provide. God *does* offer comfort to all. As such, Bachand argues, we must not expel the God of MTD as though s/he is a usurper – s/he may just be an alternative of the evangelical/post-enlightenment vision of the Trinitarian God; an alternative/resurgent understanding of God especially engaging for all of us "who swim in 'the cultural ocean of therapeutic individualism'", for "we too can feel lost and scared in this ever changing world of ours, we too seek comfort in the loving God of our Christian faith" (Bachand, 2010, p. 155 citing imagery from Smith and Denton, 2005, pp. 172–173). As Davie might put it, a therapeutic God becomes one of the "ordinary gods of [contemporary] society" (Davie, 1994, pp. 74–92).

In other words, MTD may not be as parasitic as Smith seems to suggest. It is almost as if Smith is projecting his own understanding onto MTD. However, as an academic theologian, Bachand too sees this expression of faith (MTD) as adolescent, subjective and imperfect. MTD is simply an adolescent articulation of faith, a falling short from a designated standard of theological correctness. MTD and its adherents are deemed to be immature, to have failed in some perfect projection of faith which objective, propositional, academic theology has determined. There seems to be a form of normative Christianity, creedal Christianity, doctrinal Christianity, which subjective adolescents need to learn in their growth into objective adults.

This suggests that the articulation of faith postdates its performance: in Day's language, although young people live out their faith and perform their faith, they are not yet able to articulate it appropriately. But if we are talking about 'performative belief' is this a valid distinction? Is it necessary to differentiate between adolescent faith and adult faith in a 'practice-based' belief? Should we not be using the language Beckford uses and looking for ways in which speakers display "their competence as rational 'doers' of believing in particular social settings"; where "'Doing believing' would involve the rhetorical, linguistic, and semantic 'moves' that speakers routinely make in order to 'bring off' a performance of belief' (Beckford in Cotter, 2016, pp. 102–103). How might we shift from Digital Millennials or Generation Z or all young people being seen as performers of faith but not *bona fide* composers of religious meaning? If we argue that this is the case with adolescents, are adults any less prone to such immaturity (Bachand, 2010, p. 153)?

Interestingly, the same kind of differentiation – between a subjectively articulated lived faith ("an active embodied performance of identity") and an objectively articulated normative faith – was explored by Mathew Guest's team researching *Christianity and the University Experience* (CUE) in the UK (Guest et al., 2013a). What the team found was that the overtly propositional faith of evangelical student movements often alienated other students, even those who self-designated as Christian, whose lived expression of faith ('performative belief') was not seen to be as good as an objective propositional faith (Guest et al., 2013a, pp. 207–223; Day in Cotter, 2016, pp. 112–114). Indeed, throughout the discussion of MTD, there seems to be a suggestion that such 'propositional' (or 'grown-up' or 'traditional') faith is 'better than' the performative (or 'practice-based' or 'therapeutic') faith of the adolescents and of their parents. (Bachand, 2010, p. 155).

In 2007, before Bachand's article and Day's exploration of 'performative belief', the Barna Group did some research into "what the new generation really thinks about Christianity and why it really matters" (Kinnaman and Lyons, 2007). The research was based on a series of polls of both Christians and 'outsiders' commissioned by the Barna Group which focused on the 16–29 age group – what they term the "Mosaic" generation (pp. 247–249 – in the UK this generation would be known as 'Digital Millennials'). Most of David Kinnaman's reflection on the research sets out key aspects of what he deems to be Christianity's image problem. The keyword chapter headings are self-explanatory: "Hypocritical", "Get Saved!", "Antihomosexual", "Sheltered", "Too Political" and "Judgemental". Interestingly, the majority of these words would be antithetical to the basic assertions of MTD and also to those who perform an MTD-styled faith. The keywords posit an alternative understanding of contemporary Christianity based on evangelical orthodoxy and orthopraxy which is at extreme variance to MTD.

Given this, it is not surprising that when Mosaics are asked to criticize the Church, they do so in terms that show their preference for the categories of MTD. Indeed, although Kinnaman's response is not to suggest a wholesale reinterpretation of the Gospel, he does argue in the closing chapter that Mosaics need to become more like Jesus in terms of listening, accepting, engaging, communicating and serving (pp. 201–218). Although Kinnaman does point to the times where Jesus challenges his audience on their beliefs, there is a noticeable emphasis here on an MTD-compliant Jesus – a Jesus who provides a therapeutic response to his adversaries. In turn, one reading of Kinnaman's conclusion is that I am to provide a therapeutic offer to those embroiled in MTD thinking. This is how Gabe Lyons summarizes the Christian life:

> Being Christian is hard work. Putting the needs of others above your own, loving your neighbor, doing good to those who would do evil to you, exercising humility, suffering with those less fortunate, and doing it all with a pure heart is nearly impossible. But it is Jesus' model and call.
> (p. 223)

What we have is a clear shift from evangelical, propositional certainty, an objectified faith written in terms of doctrinal absolutes, to a much more MTD-friendly faith built on a more subjective therapeutic discipleship model: therapeutic both for the individual ("a pure heart") and for society. Indeed, in the Barna Group's latest research about discipleship (published February 2016), even the term 'discipleship' is shown to be less popular than more therapeutic terms such as 'becoming more Christ-like', 'spiritual growth' and 'spiritual journey' (Barna Group, 2016b).

This all ties in with Bachand's third line of argument: faith should not be seen, after all, as an objective list of beliefs but rather as a process of "inherently developmental meaning-making" (Bachand, 2010, p. 145). In other words, it is not so much that adolescents actually have a less adequate theology than adults but rather that faith, for both adolescents and adults, is an active meaning-making process that is developmental for both. So Manuel Vásquez, commenting on Day's *Believing in Belonging*, borrows from Pierre Bourdieu (1977, p. 72) to discuss faith not as *opus operatum*, a permanent and ineffable private state of mind expressed transparently through a creed or a dogma, but rather as *modus operandi*, a dynamic process that is produced and sustained socially and that involves the totality of the person, including practices and emotions (Velasquez in Cotter, 2016, p. 109). Adolescent faith, argues Bachand, is as real and authentic as adult faith, despite its subjectivity and partial articulation. The CUE project asserts its own form of this: "religious identities cannot be simply reduced to a matter of propositional belief, conceived as coherent and cerebral, and hence vulnerable to cognitive dissonance", but rather "matters of 'belief' . . . are configured as 'believing', an active embodied performance of identity, rather than an assent to a given set of official truth claims" (Guest et al., 2013a, p. 24).

On similar grounds, Friedrich Schweitzer argues that adolescents are indeed theologians – but not the kind of theologians that we immediately assume that they need to be, namely protectors of orthodoxy and objectifiers of propositional faith (Schweitzer, 2014). Adolescent theologians are not doing the same level of task as academic theologians. Instead, both groups are "trying to make sense of ultimate questions and to understand what, for example, the idea of God really means" (Schweitzer, 2014, p. 185). Schweitzer is intentionally drawing on distinctions between academic theology and lay theology, or 'ordinary theology' in the terms of Astley and Pete Ward (Astley, 2001; Ward, 2011). In these terms, ordinary theology provides insights into a lived theology, a performed theology of the community and of individuals rather than the normative or formal theology of the academics. Adolescents, therefore, may be really good examples of ordinary theologians – "signal processors of the Spirit" (Armstrong in Astley and Francis, 2013, pp. 65–85).

However, ordinary theology isn't just the gathered opinions of the masses (Astley, 2001, pp. 138–145; Armstrong, 2013, p. 65). Astley argues that ordinary theologians have to demonstrate both "sufficient critical reflection" and "sufficient evidence of personal appropriation of beliefs" and ordinary theologians need to demonstrate a commitment to "critical dialogue with Christian sources and some reflection on practical situations and their own actions within them" (Astley, 2001, p. 142). This critical reflection, Astley argues, is part and parcel of the ordinary life of the ordinary theologian just as much as it is of the academic. Much of Schweitzer's article in fact draws a distinction between adolescent faith and academic faith: between adolescents as theologians, and adolescents as recipients of theology, and as adolescent theology as a gateway for academic theologians to engage with contemporary culture. Despite this, in the end adolescent theology does not seem to be a valid form of theological expression of itself but rather a test case for academic scrutiny (Schweitzer, 2014, p. 189).

Some potential contributory factors 101

In the central section of his article, Schweitzer argues for a distinction between theology *of* adolescents, theology *with* adolescents and theology *for* adolescents (Schweitzer, 2014, pp. 190–196). In this section, he helpfully makes use of excerpts of interviews with adolescents which show their own engagement with and development of theological reflection. Taken with Bachand's exploration of the subjectivity of adolescent theology, Schweitzer's conclusion that there needs to be a radical engagement between theology of, theology with and theology for adolescents seems to make sense. While academic, adult or normative theology will not necessarily agree with the articulation of faith made by adolescents, the only way forward would seem to be a recognition that there needs to be a dialogue between the different voices.

Of course, the issue here is not actually between adolescent and adult theology (even if such categories could be sustained), but rather between propositional or practice-based belief, or, in the terms of Theological Action Research (TAR), between normative/formal theology and espoused/operant theology (Cameron et al., 2010). So, again, in exploring the culture found in the CUE project, Guest's team noted that there is a consensus within religious organizations focused on campus engagement that propositional belief (formal/normative) is the norm – for Christians, Muslims and Secularists (Guest et al., 2013b, p. 211). Indeed, the very culture of the university experience seemed to reinforce the assumption that belief/religion is more about propositional assent (formal/normative) than about performance (espoused/operant), as I have already discussed in terms of Day's research (Day, 2010, pp. 12–14).

However, such a view seems less prevalent within contemporary explorations of practical theology, such as Astley's ordinary theology or in ARCS' TAR methodology (Astley, 2001; Cameron et al., 2010, pp. 47–60). In both of these processes, the practice of religion acts as a form of theological reification in itself: "practices of faithful Christian people are themselves already the bearers of theology; they express the contemporary living tradition of the Christian faith" (Cameron et al., 2010, p. 51). As such, TAR has developed a process of theological reflection based on four voices of theology: operant, espoused, normative and formal. These voices relate to theology in practice (operant), theology in conversation with practitioners (espoused), authorized theology (ecclesial, community, individual) and theology in the academy (formal) (Cameron et al., 2010, pp. 53–56). On the one hand, TAR can be seen as a way of applying normative theology to wayward practice – as with Schweitzer's approach to adolescent theology needing instruction/guidance. But operant and espoused theologies are as important in their own ways as faith seeking understanding. So, on the

102 *Some potential contributory factors*

other hand, TAR can also seek to question and change normative theology through the lived-out practice of religion/performative belief.

MTD is, in Smith's characterization, a lived-out version of religion, an operant faith espoused through the conversations Smith has with its teenage proponents. As such, that form of faith needs to be accepted as an authentic, mediatized, performance of belief. In this book, I am arguing that the ordinary social performance of Bible engagement in digital culture reifies faith-related convictions of social media users and tends to show them preferring to perform therapeutic verses rather than propositional verses. However, one of the intriguing factors of this performance of MTD is the way in which its adherents reflect the authority of a propositional faith when their own performative belief is reflected back to them (Smith and Denton, 2005, pp. 67–71). So, when challenged on spiritual pick and mix religion, or on the need to abandon faith, often Smith's interlocutors reflect back a more conservative explanation of their faith and of their own religious communities. Similarly, when social media users share Bible texts (intensive engagement) rather than consume them (extensive engagement), there is a greater frequency of propositional verses than in the former. Those engaging with the Bible in this way adapt their social performance when they are sharing on the social media feed/when they consciously or subconsciously consider the audience whom they are addressing. This seems to be the same kind of process which Smith is noting. When people are asked to clarify (in conversation) or when they perform to a public audience (on social media), they tend to respond with propositional answers, focusing on their own identity as Christians rather than on the kind of therapeutic texts which they explore in more extensive modes of engagement (searching, reading, listening).

Media ecology

In 2013, the Barna Group released research exploring how technology was changing the faith of Digital Millennials (Barna Group, 2013). It is a theme which media companies are keen to explore, with the BBC Future Now team publishing an article in 2015 by Chris Stokel-Walker which explored the impact of technology on the expression of faith. The Barna Group begin their article in terms of performative belief: the Church has regularly made use of "regular habits and practices designed to help people worship . . . habitual practices . . . have been part of the Church throughout the centuries" (Barna Group, 2013). Social connectivity on the internet is then said to be "reshaping personal spirituality" among younger generations, not least through social media and popular platforms such as Google, Facebook and Twitter. The main section of the article explores Bible engagement on both *YouVersion* and *BibleGateway*. The Barna Group lists figures for reading the Bible on screen (70% for Christian millennials, 33% for all millennials – I think the survey is limited to the USA), use of faith-related video and online searching of places of worship. According to the Barma Group, 14% of millennials (38% of Christian millennials) use the internet to verify something a faith leader has said; they note that large numbers seek out information and have conversations online about faith matters. When Barna Group CEO David Kinnaman comments, he talks about the need for transparency in a digital age and the suggestion that millennials are keen to check up on what leaders are saying. Kinnaman argues that churches should engage with millennials in two-way conversation, holistically integrating technology into the faith experience.

Stokel-Walker's argument goes a little further in exploring actual change in religious experience, from the use of mobile phones in cathedrals, blogging bishops and the Bible as a mobile phone app. Technology has always gone hand in hand with religious faith: the Bible has changed from scrolls, to the codex, to books, and now to apps – and all the time it also been available through art, music and voice. Moreover, Christian worship is available online, and scholars have explored the phenomenon of online churches being developed (Hutchings, 2017b). Both the Barna Group and BBC articles ask whether it is the media which is shaping the message or whether bigger social changes like MTD and the shift towards 'anthropocentric' performative belief is changing the expression of Christianity through the media. Is the introduction of digital technology itself the greater influence? Has the digital revolution inaugurated or at least enhanced a spiritual revolution? Behind all this is a much larger question about technological determinism and the social shaping of technology. Technological determinism argues that media shapes and determines the message, indeed, as Marshall McLuhan argued, the medium is the message. However, Heidi Campbell has argued for the social shaping of technology, a much more subtle process wherein religious communities seek to adapt technology to meet their own needs and purposes (Campbell, 2010).

Hutchings has argued that technology is not necessarily deterministic *per se*, but that Bible apps are designed to create a specific form of Bible reading practices: "these digital Bibles are carefully designed to train the user in traditional Evangelical Christian understandings of reading . . . and operate as carefully structured 'persuasive technologies' deploying 'procedural rhetoric'" (Hutchings, 2017a, p. 206). Hutchings sees this design process as intentional, "as a vehicle for religious socialization" and even queries the "potential for digital media to re-shape traditional relationships of power in Evangelical Christian communities". Drawing on Brian Malley's ethnographic research into evangelical Bible reading practices (Malley, 2004), Hutchings focuses on 'frequent reading' and 'personal application' of the text (Hutchings, 2017a, p. 207). In contrast, CODEC and the Barna Group's explorations of Bible-centric Digital Millennials have a different sense and different vocabulary about how these young people engage with the Bible, suggesting something more intensive, more engaged and more curious of what others (including academics) have said or are saying (Barna Group, 2015; Ford et al., 2019; Perrin, 2016).

After looking at both *YouVersion*'s Bible App and Hodder's Glo Bible as case studies for persuasive technology, Hutchings states: "My interviewees listed five motivations for their work: seeking to make the bulky printed Bible text more accessible, easier to understand, more attractive to new audiences, more frequently read, and easier to study" (Hutchings, 2017a, p. 212). Focusing on engagement, Hutchings notes *YouVersion*'s various blog posts heralding its own success. When users were asked whether having the Bible available on mobile phones encouraged them to turn to the Bible more often, 77% said "yes". The result of more frequent reading, Hutchings argues, is "to ensure that they understand the message and hear what God wants to say to them" (Hutchings, 2017a, p. 213), although not necessarily through detailed exegesis of the passages they have read. What Hutchings does not engage with is the ordinary social performance of Bible engagement on these platforms: the sheer scale of Bible reading, the immense number of plans being read and the billions of engagements. Those platforms tend to provide a short passage of scripture and an added devotional or exegetical reading from an author. Certainly, these commentaries could provide readers with a superficial and persuasive reading of the text. But this could only be determined by a careful study of the plans provided – and, as yet, no such research exists. It seems strange then to suggest that a tradition so steeped in the exposition and exegesis of the text could so easily be persuaded by a new technology to abandon these positions.

Indeed, if the general shift which I am proposing within the ordinary social performance of Bible engagement within digital culture is correct, then the Bible apps are actually a terrible example of persuasive technology or the kind of 'captology' proposed by B.J. Fogg (in Hutchings, 2017a, p. 213). Of all the lists which I have explored, *YouVersion*'s is the most 'therapeutic' in inclination. One would have expected an evangelical-designed, purposefully persuasive technology to result in popular verses which display traditional 'theocentric' or 'propositional' or 'creedal' notions. Instead, for the most part, *YouVersion*'s lists sway heavily towards the therapeutic, practice-based traditions – especially in searching, hearing and listening – in aspects of Bible consumption.

It may be that Hutchings' article is too focused on specific apps rather than exploring media ecology as a whole. As it stands, it seems to present an attempt at media ecology design which has misfired in some way. It is

Some potential contributory factors 105

true that millions of people around the world are involved in Bible reading because of *YouVersion*. However, I cannot be totally sure of who those readers are, or where they are, or whether they were already reading the Bible on a regular basis or not. *YouVersion*'s blog posts do provide headline data about world growth but never provide the hard data needed to a full analysis – and *BibleGateway* fares no better in terms of providing data for research. The problem is that my research on the ordinary social performance of Bible engagement does not suggest that the persuasive technology which Hutchings argues for is designed into these platforms and if it is, it is not effective in creating good, 'propositional', evangelical readers. It would seem that such technology is being countered by even stronger social movements, particularly the shift from propositions to performative belief.

A brief exploration of one aspect of the design process might make this point a little clearer. One of my conversation partners in developing this research, Bex Lewis, proposed that the statistics for the most popular verses may have been influenced by *YouVersion's* practice of issuing a verse of the day, which is distributed to followers through the mobile application and through a Twitter account (@Daily_Bible). Theoretically, such an activity could have influenced the data. Having contacted *YouVersion* to request information on the project, without success, I analyzed all the data for a five-month period from August 1, 2014 to December 31, 2014. I included in the data set the verse, Bible version, number of retweets, number of favourites and total number of interactions. The recording of online interactions (rather than just views) also means that this data acts as another model for online Bible engagement. What kinds of Bible verses are favourited or retweeted most?

The first thing to notice is that the scheduling of Bible verses showed minimal strategic planning during this early period. Tweets did not reflect liturgical events like Christmas, although there was a special tweet with an added image for Thanksgiving. This meant that tweets around a high point in the liturgical year had fewer interactions because they were not related to the event. So, on Christmas Eve, the daily verse was Leviticus 20:7–8 ("You shall consecrate yourselves therefore and be holy, for I am the Lord your God".), which gained 165 interactions; on Christmas Day, it was Micah 6:8 ("What he requires of you is this: to do what is just, to show constant love, and to live in humble fellowship".), which gained 266 interactions.

Of the 117 verses tweeted over the period (sometimes there were significant breaks in the regular tweeting), 24 verses (21%) received more than 300 interactions each. The verse which was engaged with the most was on Thanksgiving 2014: the text was 1 Chronicles 16:34 ("Give thanks to the Lord, for he is good; his love endures forever".) and received 760 interactions. Notably, this verse was tweeted with an attached picture – the only

106 *Some potential contributory factors*

picture distributed throughout the five-month period. The coalescence of the right text, the right picture and the right date seems to have found the sweet spot in online interactivity.

The following list gives the verses interacted with the most.

1   1 Chronicles 16:34 (November 24, 760): "Give thanks to the Lord"
2   Colossians 3:23–24 (August 14, 463): "Whatever you do, work at it with all your heart"
3   Romans 12:12 (October 2, 399): "Let your hope keep you joyful"
4   Romans 1:16 (September 14, 393): "For I am not ashamed of the gospel"
5   1 Corinthians 13:4–5 (September 26, 385): "[Love] isn't rude, it doesn't seek its own advantage"
6   Psalm 37:4 (November 19, 377): "Delight yourself in the Lord; and He will give you"
7   Proverbs 13:20 (November 20, 369): "Keep company with the wise and you will become wise"
8   James 3:17–18 (December 31, 368): "But the wisdom from above is first pure"
9   Ephesians 4:29 (December 27, 364): "Do not let any unwholesome talk come out of your mouths"
10 Psalm 18:2 (October 30, 358): "The Lord is my protector"

It is noticeable, firstly, that the first two verses in this list are also included in *YouVersion*'s most shared Bible verses list noted earlier (YVS14), but in the reverse order. Clearly the 1 Chronicles verse is almost definable as 'click-bait' – a verse and picture tweeted in such a way and on such a day (Thanksgiving) as to maximize interaction. Indeed, this seems even more the case when I think of the tweets around the Christmas holiday period that received only average interaction. You might have expected Luke 2 or John 1 on Christmas Day, with associated nativity scene, rather than verses from Leviticus and Micah.

Secondly, most of the verses provide a positive moral message in line with the elements of MTD. Indeed, I have already noted that Colossians 3:23–24 offers a distinctly MTD-type ethic. But at the same time there are verses which reflect more of a propositional approach to faith, not least Romans 1:16: "For I am not ashamed of the Gospel, for it is the power of God for salvation to everyone who believes, to the Jew first and also to the Greek". The specificities of this verse, its use of 'Gospel', 'Jews' and 'Greeks', 'the power of God' and the differentiation between those who believe and those who do not, seems to militate against the normal categories of MTD-type referencing. But I have also discussed the tendency for MTD-type Christians to hold fast to more conservative values when challenged or when

Some potential contributory factors 107

making some form of public statement. Romans 1:16 offers another such opportunity to make a distinctive Christian identity statement ("I hold fast to the Gospel") without needing to explain what that Gospel is about, without directly referring to an interventionist God.

Thirdly, it is worth noting the verses receiving the least amount of interaction are precisely those verses that challenge the core values of MTD. So, six verses gained fewer than 130 interactions:

1 James 3:9–10 (December 15, 105): "Sometimes it praises . . ., and sometimes it curses"
2 Ecclesiastes 11:5 (December 5, 111): "Just as you cannot understand the wind or the mystery of a tiny baby growing in its mother's womb"
3 Hebrews 4:15 (September 18, 117): "Our High Priest is not one who cannot feel sympathy"
4 1 Timothy 2:1–2 (September 30, 118): "Therefore I exhort first of all that supplications"
5 1 Corinthians 1:10 (October 1, 126): "Now I exhort you, brethren, by the name of our Lord Jesus Christ, that you all agree"
6 Isaiah 7:14 (Aug 18, 127): "All right then, the Lord himself will give you the sign. Look! The virgin will conceive"

We see immediately that each text militates against an MTD-type reading. The verses from James are a rather disjointed segment on the teaching about the use of the tongue and raise real issues about social conflict. The passage from Ecclesiastes raises an intriguing sense of mystery, but with current arguments raging about abortion and fertilization in both politics and religion in the USA, the reference to an unborn child may make people hesitate before retweeting (61) or favouriting (50) the verse. The verses from both Hebrews and Timothy may well have produced resistance to engagement because of their use of archaic language – the reference to High Priest and to supplications. These verses have not been translated into modern idioms or semantic equivalents, and so would raise problems for those seeking to share them with their social media communities. Indeed, this may be the same reason that 1 Corinthians 1:10 and Isaiah 7:14 also received few interactions. However, it may well be different for the former verse in that it is one of the few verses in any of these lists of popular or unpopular verses that explicitly mentions Jesus.

From a brief study of this data set then, it would appear that my findings are consistent with my study of other data sets: online engagement is preferential for MTD-type Bible verses and avoids specific mention of divine intervention or of specifics about Jesus. There are times when more propositional verses are chosen, but these verses often appear as identity markers signaling adherence to core Christian values which users think are more acceptable in Bible friendly societies like the USA.

In fact, when I talked with representatives from Bible apps at an international Bible conference, it was made clear to me that the 'verse of the day' process was initially developed on an ad hoc basis. However, more recently, the decision had been made to ensure the list reflected user data of favourite verses. In other words, a Bible app would create its own filter bubble by using user-generated data (increasingly MTD) to create a verse-of-the-day feature. If the app was being developed through a persuasive technology/'captology' model, then one would have expected a greater use of strategic application of 'propositional' verses at this point.

It would seem that there is yet more evidence that the social performance of Bible engagement is not part of a deterministic model of technological development – or if it is, other change processes are much more powerful. One of those processes, of course, may be the increasing secularization of the media itself. So, Hjarvard (2013, p. 120) talks about mediatization as "about long-term social and cultural change and as such it may be considered on par with other significant social and cultural transformative processes of high modernity, including individualisation, urbanisation, globalisation and secularisation". Indeed, he argues for an interdependence between these various processes such that "the rise and spread of communication media have in some ways been a prerequisite' for them. In other words, the media provides a way of speaking about the society in which we live, a pattern for our thinking, an example of practice-led belief. Hjarvard argues (2013, p. 121) that "usage of specific media and interpretation of various kinds of media texts play an important role for audience's construction of cultural identity and sense of public connection". In other words, for my research, if the media is becoming more focused on 'anthropocentric' and 'therapeutic' texts, then this provides a model for individuals to explore the Bible through terms of 'therapeutic' engagement rather than 'propositional'. In other words, the more society becomes secularized, the more the media which is societal will become secularized, and the more the public will be influenced by that media.

In exploring the impact of digital media on theological expression, Esther McIntosh makes a similar point. She critiques the lack of research and analysis into "the effect of mediating the Christian message through digital technology, nor the possible distortions of that message that media and especially digital media make possible" (McIntosh, 2015, p. 136). Indeed, the Church's rush to go online "is not matched by a corresponding analysis of the effects of so doing". McIntosh also notes that by rushing online, the Church does not seem to have realized that its offer is one of many online and its offer is also plural in itself. As such, digital consumers are at liberty to assign different aspects of different faiths to their own sense of spirituality.

Borrowing from Schulz, Hjarvard talks of four types of potential change:

> (1) media extend human communication and interaction beyond immediate time and space, (2) they substitute existing forms of face-to-face communication and interaction, (3) media and existing forms of communication and interaction amalgamate with one another and (4) social actors and institutions may accommodate to the logic of the media.
> (Hjarvard, 2013, p. 122)

The last of these seem to be the most pertinent here. If digital media has the potential to promote a greater sense of 'secularization', then that is most likely to influence social actors, including those engaged in Bible engagement online, to accommodate to this sense of secularization. Such accommodation could result in a decreasing number of 'propositional' verses being shared and greater number of 'therapeutic' verses being shared'. This is made even more powerful by the media's adoption of the "social functions of institutionalised religions" to "provide spiritual guidance, moral orientation, ritual passages and a sense of community and belonging" and "to define what counts as religion" (Hjarvard, 2013, pp. 124–125).

Both Hjarvard and McIntosh are encouraging the Church to think about its engagement with digital media because they are aware that digital media changes the messaging of the Church – or rather, as media consumers, 'church people' are influenced by the media to adopt the media's terms of engagement. So, since the media argues for faith as 'therapeutic', then they tend to talk in 'therapeutic' terms. However, I wonder what will happen in a 'Christian Nationalist' USA. Will it be the case that as medium normalizes the 'Trump factor' and becomes more aligned with conservative attitudes to the Bible, then will more 'propositional' texts become more popular?

The *Journal for Culture and Religion* issue which included Hjarvard's provocative exploration of media and religion also contained important articles by Lövheim, David Morgan, Lynn Schofield Clark and Alexandra Boutos, all of which are worth closer study. The contributions are brought together by Gordon Lynch in a concluding article: "What can we learn from the mediatisation of the religion debate?" (Lynch, 2011). In this article, Lynch notes that the criticisms of Hjarvard's thesis focus on the historical specificity of his argument which therefore "does not yet provide an adequate theoretical framework for thinking more generally about the relationship between religion, media and social change" (Lynch, 2012, p. 204). Moreover, some have criticized Hjarvard's tendency to elide different social and cultural movements into one – hence assuming that global capitalism

110 *Some potential contributory factors*

and digital media are both governed by the same factors, and his claim that media takes on the functions previously performed by religious institutions. Lynch notes that such arguments fit Western and Northern Europe much better than other areas of the world, including the USA and the Middle East. As such, Stewart Hoover (cited in Lynch, 2011, p. 205) notes that mediatization will take different forms in different places and "we should not expect it to be unitary along dimensions of either structure or practice". This was addressed in my earlier consideration of the kind of verses that might be shared in a 'Christian Nationalist' USA. It's already clear, in the YVP lists by country, how different verses are popular in different religious and media ecologies.

One of the most important points for this piece of research is Lynch's suggestion about the need to think about the content of the audience:

> It is necessary to identify what multiple audiences and publics are present within a given context, and in what ways public media is implicated in the reproduction of a common or fragments communicative space.
> (Lynch, 2011, p. 206)

I have already noted that the Bible platforms in my research are global. It may be that *BibleGateway* is more Anglophone and that this might affect specific national listings and a diminishing of the popularity of those verses most popular within, for example, Latin America. But I have also noted the 'ordinary' nature of this data. The numbers seem too large to be limited to one particular form of media ecology or mediatization. The data encompass both Western Europe and the USA, both Northern Europe and the Middle East. As such, the influence of media ecology on the lists would seem to be quite limited, especially in terms of Hjarvard's thesis. Instead it is likely that there are plural affects acting on the results which include the effects of digital media (Hjarvard, 2011; McIntosh, 2015; Hutchings, 2017a), but also much longer term sociological shift noted by both Day (2011) and Smith Smith and Denton (2005), among many others.

Conclusion
An ordinary canon within social media engagement?

This study explored 20 data sets (lists) from different web-based and mobile applications between 2012 and 2019, reflecting on whether verses in the lists tended to reflect broadly 'therapeutic' or 'propositional' verses – or in the terms set by Abby Day, 'anthropocentric' or 'theocentric' verses. Throughout my analysis, I have drawn an equivalence between the different terms in Christian Smith and Day. I also noted a difference between 'extensive' (searching/consuming) and 'intensive' (annotating/bookmarking/highlighting/sharing) Bible engagement online and the different modes of expression linked to these different performances in different lists.

In this study I have successfully mapped ordinary social performance of Bible engagement in digital culture against Day's concept of 'performative belief' and Smith's construal of MTD and, at the same time, noted that social media users engaging with the Bible seek to perform aspects of their own identity which could still be construed as 'propositional' in terms of theology, but 'therapeutic' in terms of content. It seems to back up the arguments of both Smith and Ruth Perrin that there is not a sense of 'pick and mix spirituality' present in such ordinary social performance of Bible engagement.

In this study I have shown, firstly, that the most engaged verses (those that have been bookmarked, highlighted or shared the most) tend to reflect 'therapeutic/anthropocentric' verses: the kind I would expect of MTD-type Christianity. They are verses that encourage and motivate social media users, and which fit well into the therapeutic sharing culture of the internet. I have also noted that in these verses, in the main, there is little explicit mention of Jesus, of his life and ministry, death and resurrection. Indeed, there is little here to do with traditional, propositional concepts of salvation at all.

Secondly, I have found that when social media users share verses with their online communities, they tend to share motivational verses within the construal of MTD. However, they also share some verses which point to their own identity within more traditional aspects of Judaeo-Christian belief and practice. In this, there seems to be a desire to share verses which mark the user out as different or to self-identify with key elements of faith identity. This practice reflects exactly a trait picked up within Smith's work of a tendency for interviewees to reflect back propositional Christianity when questioned about aspects of their faith. They identify with (espouse) traditional Christianity, while evidencing MTD through their (operant) practice.

I have noted that all of this would be broadly in agreement with what I would expect of MTD-type Christianity and broadly consonant with the trends in Day's construal of 'performative belief'. In other words, my exploration of online Bible engagement suggests that the use of social media bookmarking, highlighting and sharing reflects an increasing use of motivational and therapeutic Bible verses. I also noted this increase in a brief exploration of Google Trends data for Jeremiah 29.11 and John 3:16 which showed the former to be both twice as popular and more dynamic, and the latter to be institutionalized and in decline.

Throughout the study, I have found that very few verses explicitly refer to anything about Jesus or seem to avoid verses pointing towards an interventionist God. Since many of the organizations involved arise out of an evangelically orientated background, this is a surprising result. With the gradual introduction of data-driven filter bubbles within the internet, it is likely that the trends will continue to increase: what is popular among users tends to be recycled back to them in order to generate further popular interactivity. None of the organizations involved seem to have an active policy of influencing these trends.

Interestingly, MTD fits internet sharing culture quite well – and so I explored the potential of a media ecology link to the shift. The preference of motivational, encouraging, non-conflictual texts encourages internet engagement (retweeting, favouriting, liking, sharing). However, in this study I have not been able to determine whether MTD-type Bible engagement is a direct result of the mediatization of religion. Instead, it would seem that internet sharing culture and the engagement with digital media in general –a long with the development/refounding of the therapeutic aspects of Christianity – are related but separate phenomena. In other words, both might be traced back to contemporary societal transformation while not being mutually dependent on one other. However, it does seem likely that internet sharing culture promotes or reinforces the preference for MTD-type belief and associated life choices to ensure that Bible-centric social media users are good citizens of the global village (or global living room!). The sociology of religion, digital engagement and mediatization all seem to come together to amplify the effect.

Does this create a new ordinary canon? Clearly, a lot more research is needed to determine this – not least to gain a much bigger picture of actual

Conclusion: an ordinary canon within social media engagement? 113

Bible engagement online. We need to see the whole range of Bible verses which are being shared online over a much longer period and on specific social media platforms. This will help us move away from the parochialism of small data sets of popular verses on specific applications. However, such a study would require access to much more information and some serious computing analysis. CODEC has already engaged in a small study to look at all the verses tweeted relating to the Gospels in one day. This experiment is showing that significant material is being picked up although hardly any of the verses in this current study come from the Gospels. More needs to be done in this area.

It is clear that the ordinary social performance of Bible engagement in digital culture contains little reference to the core doctrinal traditions of the Christian Church, especially in relation to the role of Jesus and the intervention of God into the world. That alone may signal a major change in the public image and understanding of the Bible. If Jeremiah 29:11 becomes the key public message of the Bible rather than John 3:16, then arguably we will have (re)created a (re)newed understanding of Christianity based far more on Ignatius's concept of Christianity as the "cure of sick souls" or "the medicine for immortality". Some will see this as a positive realignment of Christianity away from evangelical propositional faith; this research is not meant to argue for either view.

However, this shift in Bible engagement does provide a change: it offers a new canon of scriptures which are popular online – a fragmented canon, a therapeutic canon, a canon which is broadly orientated towards performative belief. It is this canon of a relatively few verses (ten out of 30,000?) which is being search/highlighted/bookmarked and shared through millions, if not billions, of social media engagements on an annual basis. A new ordinary canon is forming, one which reflects a millennial preference for MTD, a preference to be constructive members of the digital global village.

References

Aichele, G. (2001). *The Control of Biblical Meaning: Canon as Semiotic Mechanism*. Harrisburg, PA: Trinity Press.
Alexander, L. (2006). God's Frozen Word: Canonicity and the Dilemmas of Biblical Studies Today. *Expository Times*, *117*(6), pp. 237–242.
Alvesson, M., & Willmott, H. (2002). Producing the appropriate individual: Identity regulation as organizational control. *Journal of Management Studies*, *39*(5), pp. 619–644.
American Bible Society. (2018). *State of the Bible 2018*. Retrieved from https://1s712.americanbible.org/cdn-www-ws03/uploads/content/State_of_the_Bible_2018_Report_-_Han_Solo.pdf
Armstrong, M. (2013). Ordinary Theologians as Signal Processors of the Spirit. In J. Astley and L. Francis (eds.), *Exploring Ordinary Theology*, pp. 65–85. Farnham: Ashgate Publishing.
Astley, J. (2001). *Ordinary Theology: Looking, Listening and Learning in Theology* (Explorations in Practical, Pastoral and Empirical Theology). London: Routledge.
Astley, J. (2014). *Ordinary Theology as Lay Theology: Listening to and Learning From Lay Perspectives*. Retrieved from https://humanities.exeter.ac.uk/media/universityofexeter/collegeofhumanities/theology/centreforbiblicalstudies/Astley_2014_preprint_INTAMS_2018290.pdf
Astley, J., and Francis, L. (2013). *Exploring Ordinary Theology: Everyday Christian Believing and the Church*. Farnham: Ashgate.
Bachand, S. C. (2010). Living God or Cosmic Therapist? Implications of the National Survey of Youth and Religion for Christian Religious Education. *Religious Education*, *105*(2), pp. 140–156.
Balkan, A. (2018). *The Nature of Self in the Digital Age* [blog post]. Retrieved from https://2018.ar.al/notes/the-nature-of-the-self-in-the-digital-age/
Barna Group. (2013). *How Technology Is Changing Millennial Faith* [web article] Retrieved from www.BarnaGroup.com/research/how-technology-is-changing-millennial-faith/
Barna Group. (2015). *Making Space for Millennials: A Blueprint for Your Culture, Ministry, Leadership and Facilities*. Barna Group.
Barna Group. (2016a). *The Bible in America*. Barna Group.

References

Barna Group. (2016b). *The State of Discipleship Report*. Barna Group.
Baron, N. (2015). *Words Onscreen: The Fate of Reading in a Digital World*. Oxford: Oxford University Press.
Barrett-Fox, R. (2018). A King Cyrus President: How Donald Trump's Presidency Reasserts Conservative Christians' Right to Hegemony. *Humanity and Society*, *42*(4), pp. 503–522.
Bauckham, R. (2003). *Bible and Mission: Christian Witness in a Postmodern World*. Grand Rapids, MI: Baker Academic.
Baym, N. (2010). *Personal Connections in the Digital Age*. New York, NY: Polity Press.
Baym, N., and boyd, d. (2012). Socially Mediated Publicness: An Introduction. *Journal of Broadcasting and Electronic Media*, *56*(3), pp. 320–329.
Benjamin, W. (1967). The Work of Art in the Age of Mechanical Reproduction. In W. Benjamin (ed.), *Illuminations*, pp. 217–251. New York, NY: Schocken Books.
Bennett Jana, M. (2012). *Aquinas on the Web?: Doing Theology in an Internet Age*. London: T and T Clark.
Berger, T. (2017). *@Worship: Liturgical Practices in Digital Worlds* (Liturgy, Worship and Society Series). New York, NY: Routledge.
Berlinerblau, J. (2008). *Thumpin' It: The Use and Abuse of The Bible in Today's Presidential Politics*. Louisville, KY: Westminster John Knox Press.
Berry, D. M. (ed.) (2012). *Understanding Digital Humanities*. Basingstoke: Palgrave Macmillan.
BibleGateway. (2014). 2014 in Review [blog post] Retrieved from www.biblegateway.com/year-in-review/2014/
BibleGateway. (2015). 2015 in Review [blog post] Retrieved from www.biblegateway.com/year-in-review/2015/
BibleGateway. (2016). 2016 in Review [blog post] Retrieved from www.biblegateway.com/year-in-review/2016/
BibleGateway. (2018). 2018 in Review [blog post] Retrieved from www.biblegateway.com/year-in-review/2018/
Bielo, J. (ed.) (2009). *The Social Life of Scriptures: Cross-Cultural Perspectives on Biblicism*. New Brunswick, NJ: Rutgers University Press.
Black Mirror. (2011 onwards). [video] UK: Charlie Brooker.
Bloom, H. (2006). *The American Religion* (Second Edition). New York, NY: Chu Hartley Press.
Bourdieu, P. (1977). *Outline of a Theory of Practice*. Trans. Richard Nice. Cambridge: Cambridge University Press.
Byers, A. (2014). *Theomedia: The Media of God and the Digital Age*. Cambridge: Lutterworth Press.
Cameron, H., Bhatti, D., Duce, C., Sweeney, J., and Watkins, C. (2010). *Talking About God in Practice: Theological Action Research and Practical Theology*. London: SCM Press.
Campbell, H. A. (2005). *Exploring Religious Community Online: We Are One in the Network*. New York, NY: Peter Lang.
Campbell, H. A. (2010). *When Religion Meets New Media*. London: Routledge.
Campbell, H. A. (ed.) (2013). *Digital Religion: Understanding Religious Practice in New Media Worlds*. London: Routledge.

References

Campbell, H. A., and Altenhofen, B. (2015). Methodological Challenges, Innovations and Growing Pains Digital Religion Research. In S. Cheruvallil-Contractor and S. Shakkour (eds.), *Digital Methodologies in the Sociology of Religion*, pp. 1–12. London: Bloomsbury.

Campbell, H. A., and Garner, S. (2016). *Networked Theology: Negotiating Faith in Digital Culture*. Grand Rapids, MI: Zondervan.

Carr, N. (2011). *The Shallows: How the Internet Is Changing the Way We Think, Read and Remember*. London: Atlantic Books.

Castells, M. (2012). *Networks of Outrage and Hope: Social Movements in the Internet Age*. New York, NY: Polity Press.

Cetina, K. K. (2009). The Synthetic Situation: Interactionism for a Global World. *Symbolic Interaction*, *31*(1), pp. 61–87.

Chapman, P. (2019). *Topverses.com*. Retrieved from http://topverses.com

Cheong, P. H. (2012). Twitter of Faith: Understanding Social Media Networking and Microblogging Rituals as Religious Practice. In P. H. Cheong, P. Fischer-Nielsen, S. Gelfgren, and C. Ess (eds.), *Digital Religion, Social Media and Culture: Perspectives, Practices and Futures*, pp. 191–206. New York, NY: Peter Lang.

Cheong, P. H. (2013). Authority. In H. Campbell (ed.), *Digital Religion: Understanding Religious Practice in New Media Worlds*, pp. 72–87. Abingdon: Routledge.

Cheong, P. H. (2014). Tweet the Message? Religious Authority and Social Media Innovation. *Journal for Religion, Media and Culture*, *3*(3), pp. 1–19.

Cheong, P. H. (2016). Religious Authority and Social Media Branding in a Culture of Religious Celebrification. In S. Hoover (ed.), *The Media and Religious Authority*, pp. 81–104. Pennsylvania, PA: Penn State University Press.

Cheruvallil-Contractor, S., and Shakkour, S. (eds.) (2015). *Digital Methodologies in the Sociology of Religion*. London: Bloomsbury.

Christensson, P. (2006). *Cyberspace Definition*. Retrieved 2019, February 5, from https://techterms.com

Collins, M. (2015). Loss of the Bible and the Bible in Lost: Biblical Literacy and Mainstream Television. In K. B. Edwards (ed.), *Rethinking Biblical Literacy*, pp. 71–94. London: Bloomsbury.

Collins-Mayo, S., and Beaudoin, T. (2010). Religion, Pop Culture, and 'Virtual Faith'. In S. Collins-Mayo and P. Dandelion (eds.), *Religion and Youth*. Aldershot: Ashgate.

Collins-Mayo, S., Mayo, B., Nash, S., and Coxsworth, C. (2010). *The Faith of Generation Y (Explorations)*. London: Church House Publishing.

Condone, S. (2014). Megachurch Pastor Twitter Activity: An Analysis of Rick Warren and Andy Stanley, Two of America's Social Pastors. *Journal for Religion, Media and Culture*, *3*(2), pp. 1–32.

Conover, M., Ratkiewicz, J., Francisco, M. R., Gonçalves, B., Menczer, F., and Flammini, A. (2011). Political Polarization on Twitter. *Icwsm*, *133*, pp. 89–96.

Coogler, R., et al., Buena Vista Home Entertainment (Firm) (2018). *Black Panther*.

Cotter, C. R., Davie, G., Beckford, J. A., Chattoo, S., Lövheim, M., Manuel, A., Vásquez, M. A., and Day, A. (2016). Around Abby Day's Believing in Belonging: Belief and Social Identity in the Modern World. In *Religion and Society: Advances in Research 7*, pp. 97–115. New York, NY: Berghahn Books.

Crockett, M. (2017). Moral Outrage in a Digital Age. *Journal of Nature Human Behaviour*, *1*, pp. 769–771.

Crossley, J. G. (2011). Biblical Literacy and the English King James Liberal Bible: A Twenty-First Century Tale of Capitalism, Nationalism and Nostalgia. *Postscripts*, *7*(2), pp. 197–211.
Crouch, A. (2017). *The Tech-Wise Family: Everyday Steps for Putting Technology in Its Proper Place*. Grand Rapids, MI: Baker Books.
Cusack, C. (2011). Some Recent Trends in the Study of Religion and Youth. *Journal of Religious History*, *35*(3), pp. 409–418.
Davie, G. (1994). *Religion in Britain Since 1945: Believing Without Belonging*. Oxford: Blackwell.
Davie, G. (2000). *Religion in Modern Europe: A Memory Mutates*. New York, NY: Oxford University Press.
Davie, G. (2017). *Religion in Public Life: Levelling the Ground*. London: Theos. Retrieved from www.theosthinktank.co.uk/cmsfiles/Reportfiles/RELIGION.PDF
Davis, E. F., and Hayes, R. B. (eds.) (2003). *The Art of Reading Scripture*. Grand Rapids, MI: Wm. B. Eerdmans.
Day, A. (2010). Propositions and Performativity: Relocating Belief in the Social. *Culture and Religion*, *111*(1), pp. 9–30.
Day, A. (2011). *Believing in Belonging: Belief and Social Identity in the Modern World*. Oxford: Oxford University Press.
de Certeau, M. (1984). *The Practice of Everyday Life*. Trans. S. Rendall. Berkeley, CA: University of California Press.
Dehaene, S. (2009). *Reading in the Brain: The New Science of How We Read*. New York, NY: Penguin.
de Lamartine, A. (1854–6). *Memoirs of Celebrated Characters* (Vols. 1–3). New York, NY: Harper and Bros. Retrieved from https://archive.org/details/memoirsofceleb02lama
Dyer, J. C. (2011). *From the Garden to the City: The Redeeming and Corrupting Power of Technology*. Grand Rapids, MI: Kregel Press.
Edwards, K. B. (2015). *Rethinking Biblical Literacy*. London: Bloomsbury.
Eliot, T. S. (1956). *On Poetry and Poets*. London: Faber and Faber.
Erasmus Roterodamus, D., *Paraclesis*, (1516). In *Desiderius Erasmus Roterodamus: Ausgewählte Werke*, ed. Hajo Holborn, Munich, 1933, 139–149.
Ferrell, L. A. (2008). *The Bible and the People*. New Haven, CT: Yale University Press.
Field, C. (2011). *Influence of the Bible* [blog post]. Retrieved from www.brin.ac.uk/influence-of-the-Bible/
Field, C. (2014). Is the Bible Becoming a Closed Book? British Opinion Poll Evidence. *Journal of Contemporary Religion*, pp. 503–528.
Ford, D. G. (2018). *Reading the Bible Outside the Church*. Eugene, OR: Pickwick Press.
Ford, D. G., Mann, J. L., and Phillips, P. M. (2019). *The Bible and Digital Millennials* (Routledge Focus on Religion). London: Routledge Press.
Gellel, A.-M. (2013). Popular Music as a Resource for the Religious Education Classroom: A Study Through Lady Gaga's Judas. *Religious Education Journal of Australia*, *29*(1), pp. 28–33.
Genette, G. (1997). *Paratexts: Thresholds of Interpretation*. Cambridge: Cambridge University Press.

Gibson, W. (1984). *Neuromancer*. London: Victor Gollancz.
Gibson, W. (2010). *Google's Earth* [web article]. Retrieved from www.nytimes.com/2010/09/01/opinion/01gibson.html
Goff, P., Farnsley II, A. E., and Thuesen, P. J. (eds.) (2017). *The Bible in American Life*. New York, NY: Oxford University Press.
Goffman, E. (1959). *The Presentation of Self in Everyday Life*. New York, NY: Doubleday.
Goffman, E. (1963). *Behaviour in Public Spaces*. New York, NY: Free Press.
Gorski, P. S. (2010). *Civil Religion Today* (ARDA Guiding Paper Series). State College, PA: The Association of Religion Data Archives at The Pennsylvania State University. Retrieved from www.thearda.com/rrh/papers/guidingpapers.asp
Gorski, P. S. (2017a). Why Evangelicals Voted for Trump: A Critical Cultural Sociology. *American Journal of Cultural Sociology*, *5*. Retrieved from www.researchgate.net/publication/318794810_Why_evangelicals_voted_for_Trump_A_critical_cultural_sociology
Gorski, P. S. (2017b). *American Covenant: A History of Civil Religion From the Puritans to the Present*. Princeton, NJ: Princeton University Press.
Guest, M., Aune, K., Sharma, S., and Warner, R. (2013a). *Christianity and the University Experience*. London: Bloomsbury.
Guest, M., Sharma, S., Aune, K., and Warner, R. (2013b). Challenging 'Belief' and the Evangelical Bias: Student Christianity in English Universities. *Journal of Contemporary Religion*, *28*(2), pp. 207–223.
Heelas, P., and Woodhead, L. (2005). *The Spiritual Revolution: Why Religion Is Giving Way to Spirituality*. Malden, MA: Blackwell.
Heidegger, M. (1977). *The Question Concerning Technology*. Trans. W. Lovitt. New York, NY: Garland Publishing.
Helland, C. (2001). Online-Religion/Religion-Online and Virtual Communities. In D. Bromley, D. E. Cowan, and J. K. Hadden (eds.), *Religion on the Internet: Research Prospects and Promises*, pp. 205–223. New York, NY: JAI Press.
Helland, C. (2005). Online Religion as Lived Religion: Methodological Issues in the Study of Religious Participation on the Internet. *Online-Heidelberg Journal of Religions on the Internet*, *1*(1). Retrieved from http://archiv.ub.uni-heidelberg.de/volltextserver/volltexte/2005/5823/
Helland, C. (2012). *Scholar's Top 5: Christopher Helland on Online Religion and Religion Online*, NMRDC Blog Series. Retrieved from https://digitalreligion.tamu.edu/blog/mon-05142012-1132/scholar's-top-5-christopher-helland-online-religion-and-religion-online
Hine, C. (2015). *Ethnography for the Internet: Embedded, Embodied and Everyday*. London: Bloomsbury.
Hjarvard, S. (2011). The Mediatisation of Religion: Theorising Religion, Media and Social Change. *Culture and Religion*, *12*(2), pp. 119–135.
Hjarvard, S. (2013). *The Mediatization of Culture and Society*. London: Routledge.
Hogan, B. (2010). The Presentation of Self in the Age of Social Media: Distinguishing Performances and Exhibitions Online. *Bulletin of Science, Technology and Society*, *30*(6), pp. 377–386.

References

Hughes, P. (2013a). *Putting Life Together*. Sydney: Australian Bible Society.
Hughes, P. (2013b). Bible Engagement Among Australian Young People. In A. Blenkinsop (ed.), *The Bible According to Gen Z*. Australian Bible Society [online].
Hunt, E. (2019*). Faking It: How Selfie Dysmorphia Is Driving People to Seek Surgery* [article]. Retrieved from www.theguardian.com/lifeandstyle/2019/jan/23/faking-it-how-selfie-dysmorphia-is-driving-people-to-seek-surgery
Hutchings, T. R. B. (2013). Christianity and Digital Media. In S. D. Brunn (ed.), *The Changing World Religion Map: Sacred Places, Identities, Practices and Politics*, pp. 3811–3830. New York, NY: Springer Publications.
Hutchings, T. R. B. (2014). Now the Bible Is an App: Digital Media and Changing Patterns of Religious Authority. In K. Granholm, M. Moberg, and S. Sjö (eds.), *Religion, Media and Social Change*, Chapter 9, pp. 143–161. London: Routledge.
Hutchings, T. R. B. (2015). E-Reading and the Christian Bible. *Studies in Religion/Sciences Religieuses*, *44*(4), pp. 423–440.
Hutchings, T. R. B. (2017a). Design and the Digital Bible: Persuasive Technology and Religious Reading. *Journal of Contemporary Religion*, *32*(2), pp. 205–219.
Hutchings, T. R. B. (2017b). Creating Church Online: Ritual, Community and New Media. London: Routledge Press.
Kalogridis, L. (Creator) (2018). *Altered Carbon* [Television Series]. Retrieved from www.netflix.com
Keener, C. (2017). *On the Non-Trump Evangelicals* [web article]. Retrieved from www.huffingtonpost.com/entry/on-the-non-trump-evangelicals_us_59d5a494e4 b0666ad0c3cac4?guccounter=1
Keown, G. L., Scalise, P. J., and Smothers, T. G. (1995). *Word Biblical Commentaries: Jeremiah 26–52*. Dallas, TX: Word Books.
KingJamesOnline (2013). *10 Most Popular Bible Verses of 2012*. Retrieved from http://kingjamesonline.org/most-popular-Bible-verses-of-2012/
Kinnaman, D., and Lyons, G. (2007). *UnChristian*. Grand Rapids, MI: Baker Books.
Kirschenbaum, M., and Werner, S. (2014). Digital Scholarship and Digital Studies: The State of the Discipline. *Book History*, *17*(1), pp. 406–458. Johns Hopkins University Press.
Lawrence, L. J. (2009). *The Word in Place: Reading the New Testament in Contemporary Contexts*. London: SPCK.
Lee, M. (2014). *150 Million Bible Readers Were Searching for Love Most in 2014* [web article]. Retrieved from www.christianitytoday.com/news/2014/december/150-million-Bible-readers-searching-for-love-Bible-gateway.html
Lindbeck, G. (2002). Towards a Postliberal Theology. In J. Buckley (ed.), *The Church in a Postliberal Age: George A. Lindbeck (Radical Traditions)*. London: SCM Press.
Liu, Z. (2008). *Paper to Digital: Documents in the Information Age*. Westport, CT: Libraries Unlimited.
Lundbom, J. (2004). *Anchor Bible Commentaries: Jeremiah 21–36*. New York, NY: Doubleday.
Lynch, G. (2011). What Can We Learn From the Mediatisation of Religion Debate? *Culture and Religion*, *12*(2), pp. 203–210.
Lynch, J. (2012). *The Scent of Lemons: Technology and Relationships in the Age of Facebook*. London: Darton, Longman and Todd.

Malley, B. (2004). *How the Bible Works: An Anthropological Study of Evangelical Biblicism*. Washington, DC: AltaMira.
Malley, B. (2009). Understanding the Bible's Influence. In J. Bielo (ed.), *The Social Life of Scriptures: Cross-Cultural Perspectives on Biblicism*, pp. 194–204. New Brunswick, NJ: Rutgers University Press.
Marwick, A., and boyd, d. (2010). I Tweet Honestly, I Tweet Passionately: Twitter Users, Context Collapse, and the Imagined Audience. *New Media and Society*, *13*(1), pp. 114–133.
Marwick, A., and boyd, d. (2011). To See and Be Seen: Celebrity Practice on Twitter. *Convergence*, *17*(2), pp. 139–158.
Mason, M., Singleton, A., and Webber, R. (2005) *'The Spirit of Generation Y' – The Spirituality of Australian Youth and Young People Aged 13–29* [online report]. Retrieved from https://resource.acu.edu.au/mmason/sppub/sppub.html
McConnell, F. (1986). *The Bible and the Narrative Tradition*. Oxford: Oxford University Press.
McIntosh, E. (2015). Belonging Without Believing: Church as Community in an Age of Digital Media. *International Journal of Public Theology*, *9*, pp. 131–155.
Meredith, C. (2015). A Big Room for Poo: Eddie Izzard's Bible and the Literacy of Laughter. In K. B. Edwards (ed.), *Rethinking Biblical Literacy*, pp. 187–211. London: Bloomsbury.
Michel, J. B., Shen, Y. K., Aiden, A. P., Veres, A., Gray, M. K., Brockman, W., The Google Books Team, Pickett, J. P., Hoiberg, D., Clancy, D., Norvig, P., Orwant, J., Pinker, S., Nowak, M. A., and Aiden, E. L. (2010). Quantitative Analysis of Culture Using Millions of Digitized Books. *Science Journal*. Retrieved from http://books.google.com/ngrams
Mirani, L. (2014). *The Future of Mobile Phones Doesn't Include Phone Calls* [web article]. Retrieved from https://qz.com/216148/the-future-of-mobile-phones-doesnt-include-phone-calls/
Murthy, D. (2013). *Twitter: Digital Media and Society Series*. Cambridge: Polity Press.
Myles, R. (2015). Biblical Literacy and the Simpsons. In K. B. Edwards (ed.), *Rethinking Biblical Literacy*, pp. 143–162. London: Bloomsbury.
Network for New Media, Religion and Digital Culture Studies (NNMRDC) (2019). *Network for New Media, Religion and Digital Culture Studies* [website]. Retrieved from https://digitalreligion.tamu.edu
Nikolev, D., Oliveira, D. F. M., Flammini, A., and Menczer, F. (2015). Measuring Online Social Bubbles. *PeerJ Computer Science*, *1*(e38). https://doi.org/10.7717/peerj-cs.38
Noll, M. A. (2015). *In the Beginning Was the Word: The Bible in American Public Life, 1492–1783*. New York, NY: Oxford University Press.
Noll, M. A. (2017). The Bible: Then and Now. In P. Goff, A. E. Farnsley II, and P. J. Thuesen (eds.), *The Bible in American Life*, pp. 331–344. New York, NY: Oxford University Press.
OfCom. (2018). *A Decade of Digital Dependency* [web article]. Retrieved from www.ofcom.org.uk/about-ofcom/latest/features-and-news/decade-of-digital-dependency
Olin, J. C. (tr.) (1987). *Christian Humanism and the Reformation*, pp. 97–108. New Haven, CT: Yale University Press.

References

Paauw, G. R. (2016). *Saving the Bible From Ourselves: Learning to Read and Live the Bible Well*. Downers Grove, IL: InterVarsity Press.
Perrin, R. H. (2016). *The Bible Reading of Young Evangelicals*. Eugene, OR: Pickwick Press.
Petersen, J. (2013). *2013 Year in Review on Bible Gateway* [web article]. Retrieved from www.biblegateway.com/blog/2013/12/2013-year-in-review-on-Bible-gateway/
Pew Research Centre. (2018) *Social Media Factsheet* [web article]. Retrieved from www.pewinternet.org/fact-sheet/social-media/
Phillips, P. M. (2016). *Which Lazarus Was Bowie Really Referring to in His Mesmerising Swan Song?* Retrieved from http://theconversation.com/which-lazarus-was-bowie-really-referring-to-in-his-mesmerising-swan-song-53127
Phillips, P. M. (2017). *Engaging the Word: Biblical Literacy and Christain Discipleship*, Abingdon: Bible Reading Fellowship.
Phillips, P. M. (2018). The Pixelated Text: Reading the Bible Within Digital Culture. *Theology, 121*(6), pp. 403–412.
Phillips, P. M. (2019). The Power of Visual Culture and the Fragility of the Text. In D. Hamidović, C. Clivaz, and S. B. Savant (eds.), *Ancient Manuscripts in Digital Culture: Visualisation, Data Mining, Communication*, pp. 30–49. Brill.
Phillips, P. M. (in press). Depicting 'Biblical' Narratives: A Test Case on Noah. In W. Clayton (ed.), *The Bible Onscreen in the New Millennium*. Manchester: Manchester University Press.
Phillips, P. M., Schiefelbein-Guerrero, K., and Kurlberg, J. (2019). Defining Digital Theology: Digital Humanities, Digital Religion and the Particular Work of the CODEC Research Centre and Network. *Open Theology* 5(1), pp. 29–43.
Pink, S., Horst, H., Postill, J., Hjorth, L., Lewis, T., and Tacchi, J. (2016). *Digital Ethnography: Principles and Practice*. London: Sage Publications.
Poleg, E. (2013). *Approaching the Bible in Medieval England*. Manchester: Manchester University Press.
Powery, E. B. (2017). The Origins of Whiteness and the Black (Biblical) Imagination: The Bible in the "Slave Narrative" Tradition. In P. Goff, A. E. Farnsley II, and P. J. Thuesen (eds.), *The Bible in American Life*, pp. 81–88. New York, NY: Oxford University Press.
Price, D., and Ryrie, C. C. (2004). *Let It Go Among Our People: An Illustrated History of the English Bible From John Wyclif to the King James Version*. Cambridge: Lutterworth Press.
Pyper, H. (1998). The Selfish Text: The Bible and Memetics. In C. Exum and S. Moore (eds.), *Bible Studies/Cultural Studies: The Third Sheffield Colloquium*. Sheffield: Sheffield Academic Press.
Rau, A. (2014). *How We Read the Bible: Bible Gateway's 2014 Year in Review* [blog post]. Retrieved from www.biblegateway.com/blog/2014/12/how-we-read-the-Bible-Bible-gateway-releases-its-2014-year-in-review/
Rau, A. (2015a). *The Top Ten Bible Verses of 2015 and More: Bible Gateway's Year in Review Is Here* [blog post]. Retrieved from www.biblegateway.com/blog/2015/12/the-top-ten-Bible-verses-of-2015-and-more-Bible-gateways-year-in-review-is-here/
Rau, A. (2015b). *Bible on Demand: What 160 Million People Searched Scripture For in 2015* [web article]. Retrieved from www.christianitytoday.com/gleanings/2015/

december/Bible-on-demand-what-160-million-searched-Bible-gateway. html
Rodman, R. C. (2009). 'We Are Anglicans, They Are the Church of England': Uses of Scripture in the Anglican Crisis. In James Bielo (ed.), *The Social Life of Scriptures: Cross-Cultural Perspectives on Biblicism*, pp. 100–113. New Brunswick, NJ: Rutgers University Press.
Rogers, A. P. (2015). *Congregational Hermeneutics: How Do We Read? Explorations in Practical, Pastoral and Empirical Theology*. Farnham: Ashgate Press.
Rogers, R. (2014). Debanalising Twitter: The Transformation of an Object of Study. In Weller et al. (eds.), *Twitter and Society*. New York, NY: Peter Lang.
Rojek, C. (2016). *Presumed Intimacy: Para-Social Relationships in Media, Society and Celebrity Culture*. Cambridge: Polity Press.
Sargeant, P., and Tagg, C. (2014). *The Language of Social Media: Identity and Community on the Internet*. Basingstoke: Palgrave Macmillan.
Schweitzer, F. (2014). Adolescents as Theologians: A New Approach to Christian Education and Youth Ministry. *Religious Education*, *109*(2), pp. 184–200.
Scott, L. (2016). *The Four-Dimensional Human: Ways of Being in the Digital World*. New York, NY: W. W. Norton and Company.
Selby, G. S. (2008). *Martin Luther King and the Rhetoric of Freedom: The Exodus Narrative in America's Struggle for Civil Rights*. Waco, TX: Baylor University Press.
Sherwood, Y. (2000). *A Biblical Text and Its Afterlives: The Survival of Jonah in Western Culture*. Cambridge: Cambridge University Press.
Siker, J. S. (2017). *Liquid Scripture: The Bible in a Digital World*. Minneapolis, MN: Fortress Press.
Smith, C., and Denton, M. L. (2005). *Soul Searching: The Religious and Spiritual Lives of American Teenagers*. New York, NY: Oxford University Press.
Smith, S. (2014). The Bible on Twitter in 2014 [blog post]. Retrieved from www. openbible.info/blog/2014/12/Bible-on-twitter-in-2014/
Smith, S. (2015). The Bible on Twitter in 2015 [blog post]. Retrieved from www. openbible.info/blog/2015/12/the-Bible-on-twitter-in-2015/
Stahlberg, L. C. (2008). *Sustaining Fictions: Intertextuality, Midrash, Translation and the Literary Afterlife of the Bible* (Library of Biblical Studies, 486). New York, NY: TandT Clark.
Steffan, M. (2013). Web's Most Popular Bible Verses Match Up – Except John 3:16 [web article]. Retrieved from www.christianitytoday.com/news/2013/january/webs-most-popular-Bible-verses-match-upmdashexcept-john-316.html
Stetzer, E. (2018). *Christians in the Age of Outrage: How to Bring Our Best When the World Is at Its Worst*. Carol Stream, IL: Tyndale Momentum.
Stokel-Walker, C. (2015). How Smartphones and Social Media Are Changing Christianity [web article]. Retrieved from www.bbc.com/future/story/20170222-how-smartphones-and-social-media-are-changing-religion
Storm, I., and Voas, D. (2012). The Intergenerational Transmission of Religious Service Attendance. *Nordic Journal of Religion and Society*, *25*(2), pp. 131–150.
Stulman, L. (2005). *Jeremiah*. Nashville, TN: Abingdon Press.
Taylor, P. (2017). *The Next America: Boomers, Millennials, and the Looming Generational Showdown*. New York, NY: Public Affairs.

Theissen, G. (2007). *The Bible and Contemporary Culture*. Minneapolis, MN: Fortress Press.

Turkle, S. (2016). *Reclaiming Conversation: The Power of Talk in a Digital Age*. New York, NY: Penguin.

Turner, T. (2014). *Stop Taking Jeremiah 29:11 Out of Context* [web article]. Retrieved from www.relevantmagazine.com/god/practical-faith/stop-taking-jeremiah-2911-out-context

United Bible Society. (2017). *10 Most Popular Bible Verses 2017 on Digital Bible* [web article]. Retrieved from www.unitedbiblesocieties.org/10-most-popular-Bible-verses-2017-on-digital-Bible/

Varis, P., and Blommaert, J. (2017, June). Convivialty and Collective on Social Media: Virality, Memes and New Social Structures. *Multilingual Margins*, pp. 31–45.

Village, A. (2007). *The Bible and Lay People: An Empirical Approach to Ordinary Hermeneutics* (Explorations in Practical, Pastoral and Empirical Theology). Farnham: Ashgate Press.

Wallström, M., Esmail, S., Malek, R., Slater, C., Chaikin, C., and Doubleday, P. (2016–2018). *Mr. Robot: Seasons 1–3*. Universal Studios.

Ward, G. (1997). A Guide to Theological Thinking in Cyberspace. In *Postmodern God: A Theological Reader*, pp. xv–xliii. Oxford: Blackwell.

Ward, P. (ed.) (2011). *Perspectives on Ecclesiology and Ethnography*. Grand Rapids, MI: Eerdmans.

We Are Social. (2018). *Digital in 2018* [web article]. Retrieved from https://wearesocial.com/blog/2018/01/global-digital-report-2018

Weaver, J. B. (2017a). Transforming Practice: American Bible Reading in Digital Culture. In P. Goff, A. E. Farnsley II, and P. J. Thuesen (eds.), *The Bible in American Life*, pp. 249–255. New York, NY: Oxford University Press.

Weaver, J. B. (2017b). The Bible in Digital Culture. In P. Gutjah (ed.), *The Oxford Handbook of the Bible in America*, pp. 149–162. Oxford: Oxford University Press.

Weber, K. (2013). *Sorry, John 3:16: The Top 10 Bible Verses YouVersion Shared Most in 2013* [web article]. Retrieved from www.christianitytoday.com/news/2013/december/sorry-john-316-youversion-top-10-Bible-verses-shared-most.html

Weller, K., Bruns, A., Burgess, J., Mahrt, M., and Puschmann, C. (eds.) (2014). *Twitter and Society*. New York, NY: Peter Lang.

Whitehead, A. L., Perry, S. L., and Baker, J. O. (2018). Make America Christian Again: Christian Nationalism and Voting for Donald Trump in the 2016 Presidential Election. *Sociology of Religion*, *79*(2), pp. 147–171.

Wimbush, V. L. (2012). *African Americans and the Bible: Sacred Texts and Social Textures*. Reprint Edition. Eugene, OR: Wipf & Stock.

Wochlin, M. (2005). *Bible Literacy Report: What Do American Teens Need to Know and What Do They Know*. Fairfax, VA: Bible Literacy Project.

Woodhead, L. (2007). Why so many women in holistic spirituality? A puzzle revisited. In K. Flanagan & P.C. Jupp (eds.), *A Sociology of Spirituality*, pp. 115–126, Aldershot: Ashgate Publishing.

Wolf, M. (2008). *Proust and the Squid: The Story and Science of the Reading Brain*. Thriplow: Icon Press.

Wright, B. J. (2017). *Communal Reading in the Time of Jesus: A Window Into Early Christian Reading Practices*. Minneapolis, MN: Fortress Press.

Wuthnow, R. (1994). *Sharing the Journey: Support Groups and America's New Quest for Community*. New York, NY: Free Press.

YouVersion. (2013). *Our Year With the Bible Infographic 2013* [web article]. Retrieved from http://blog.youversion.com/2013/12/our-year-with-the-Bible-infographic/

YouVersion. (2014). *Our Year With the Bible Infographic 2014* [web article]. Retrieved from http://blog.youversion.com/2014/12/our-year-with-the-Bible-infographic-2014/

YouVersion. (2015). *200 Million Installs* [web article]. Retrieved from http://installs.youversion.com/200million/index.html

YouVersion. (2017a). *Your Biggest Year Ever* [web article]. Retrieved from http://blog.youversion.com/2016/12/your-biggest-year-ever-again/

YouVersion. (2017b). *2017 Year in Review* [web article]. Retrieved from http://installs.youversion.com/2017-year-in-review/index.html

YouVersion. (2019). *The Bible App: End of the Year, 2018* [web article]. Retrieved from https://share.Bible.com/2018/

Zylstra, S. E. (2014). *Sorry Again, John 3:16: The World's 10 Most Popular Bible Verses of 2014* [web article]. Retrieved from www.christianitytoday.com/news/2014/december/worlds-10-most-popular-Bible-verses-youversion-2014.html

Zylstra, S. E. (2015). *The World's Most Popular Bible Verses, According to 200 Million YouVersion Users* [web article]. Retrieved from www.christianitytoday.com/news/2015/december/most-popular-Bible-verses-200-million-youversion-app-2015.html

Index

Note: Page numbers in italics indicate figures and in bold indicate tables on the corresponding pages.

absent-present social presence 28, 30
adolescent faith 96–98, 100; theology *of, with, and for* 101
adolescents, subjective turn in 96–97
Aeneid 6
'afterlives' of the Bible 10
Aichele, G. 10
Altenhofen, B. 25
American Bible engagement 12–19
American Bible Society 13
American Religion, The 94
anthropocentric verses 36, 69, 75–80, 88, 93, 104, 111–112
anxiety in social media user 30–31
Aronofsky, D. 11
Astley, J. 3, 96, 100
authoritative discourse, Bible as 14

Bachand, S. C. 97
backstage 30
backstage anxiety 30
banality on social media 27, 28
Barna Group **44**, 44–45, 98–99, 102–104
Baym, N. 28, 31
Beckford, J. 2, 35, 91
belief(s): "doing" 2; lived out within wider social context 2; performative 2, 35, 72, 85–86, 88, 93–95, 111; propositional 1–2, 4, 85, 88, 91–92, 108; seven dimensions model of 2–3; without belonging 1
Believing in Belonging 1, 91, 99

Benjamin, W. 31
Berger, T. 24, 25
Berlinerblau, J. 13, 14–15
Berry, D. 25
Bible, the: as authoritative discourse 14; Christendom and 7; as closed text 9; cultural reception of 10–11; decline of Bible-centrism and 11–12; in digital culture 21–22 (*see also* social media); historical importance of 6–19; mediated presence of 9; the Reformation and 8; *see also* Bible engagement
Bible and Digital Millennials, The 45
Bible-centrism 11–12, 69, 104
Bible engagement 17; American 12–16; among Digital Millennials 11, 12; anthropocentric vs. theocentric conversations on 36, 69, 75–80, 88, 93, 104, 111–112; Biblicism and 17–18; Contextual Bible Study movement 18–19; intensive lists and social performance of 82–84; moralistic therapeutic deism (MTD) in 17, 35–36, 42, 44, 78, 83–84, 85, 88, 111–112; ordinary social performance of 4, 36–37, 79, 111; pick and mix spirituality 102, 111; sample of longitudinal, in social media in English 42–45, **43**, **44**; on social media (*see* social media); in the UK 11–12, 13; *see also* Bible, the
BibleGateway: analysis and reflection on shared verses 72–79, **73**, *74*, **77**;

shared Bible verses on 34, 43, 45, 62, 63n4, 64, 69, 88, 102, 110
Bible in American Life, The 15, 44
Bible mediation 8
Bible Society 11
Bible verses, analysis and reflection of shared: BGA15, BGA16 75–79, **77**; BGP13-18 72–75, **73**, *74*; Google Trends and 86–88, *87*; intensive lists and social performance and 82–84; lists representing active social sharing (YVS14-15, OB14-15, OBRT15) 79–82; performative belief and 85–86; YVP13-18 64–72, **65–67**
Bible verses, shared 35–38; aggregating the lists of 60–62, **61**; control sample of longitudinal Bible engagement in books printed in English and 38–42, *41*; different lists of 45–60; intensive lists and social performance 82–84; sample of longitudinal Bible engagement in social media in English and 42–45, **43**, **44**
Biblical literacy 8; decline of 11–12
Biblicism 17–18
Bielo, J. 17, 18
Bloom, H. 94
Bourdieu, P. 99
Boutos, A. 109
Bowie, D. 11
boyd, d. 28, 30, 31
Bush, G. W. 14

'calling forth' 28
Campbell, H. 3, 25
celebrity culture 80–82
Cetina, K. K. 30
Chapman, P. 38–39
Cheong, P. H. 3, 22–24, 25, 32
Choi, S. 81
Christianity: Bible in development of 7; Evangelical 13–15, 103; moralistic therapeutic deism (MTD)-type 86, 92–102; nationalism and 14, 15, 109–110
Christianity and the University Experience (CUE) 98
Christianity Today 64, 69
Clark, L. S. 109
closed text, Bible as 9

CODEC Research Centre, Durham University 11, 12, 25, 44, 69, 113
Collins, M. 9–10
context collapse 31
Contextual Bible Study movement 18–19
co-present performance 30
Corpus Linguistics search tool, BYU 40
Cotter, C. R. 2–3
Crossley, J. 12
cultural homogeneity 2, 26
cultural reception of the Bible 10–11
Cusack, C. 94
cyberspace: definition of 20; different experiences in 20–21; eversion of 21

Dallas, C. 81
Davie, G. 1, 36, 92
Day, A. 1–4, 16, 17, 23, 85, 93, 110; on anthropocentric vs. theocentric conversations 36; on cultural homogeneity 26; on performative belief 2, 35, 72, 88, 93–95, 111
D-Church 24
de Certeau, M. 3
de Lamartine, A. 7–8
Denton, M. L. 4, 95
Diaz-Ortiz, C. 24
Digital Humanities 25
Digital Methodologies in the Sociology of Religion 25
Digital Millennials 11, 12, 98; development of different tribes of 21; media ecology and faith of 102–110; shift toward moralistic therapeutic deism (MTD) in 92, 111–112; strength of social media engagement among educated, urban/suburban 37
Digital Religion 25
Douglas, M. 1
'drawing out' 28
Durkheim, E. 1–2

Eckhert, M. 9
Eliot, T. S. 6, 8
Erasmus 8, 9
Evangelical Christianity 13–15, 103
eversion of cyberspace 21
exhibition space, social media as 30, 31–32

Facebook 24, 102; as exhibition space 32
faith: adolescent 96–98, 100; media ecology and changing 102–110; practice-based 96–98, 101–102, 108; as process of inherently developmental meaning-making 99–100
Field, C. 11–12, 13, 14
front stage 30

Gaga, Lady 10–11
Generation Z 94, 98
Gibson, W. 20
Glo Bible 104
Goff, P. 16
Goffman, E. 28, 30–31, 33–34
Google 102
Google Ngrams 40, 44
Google Trends 86–88, 87, 91
Gorski, P. 14
Guest, M. 98, 101
Gutenberg, J. 7, 8
Gutjahr, P. 16

happy midi-narrative 17, 92
Heelas, S. 4, 36, 42, 92, 93
Helland, C. 25
hermeneutics of presence 19
Hernandez, A. B. 81
Hine, C. 20
Hjarvard, S. 27, 92, 108, 109
Hogan, B. 30–31
Homer 6
Hughes, P. 94
Hunt, E. 29
Hutchings, T. 43, 92, 103, 104

Ignatius of Antioch 96
impression management 30
intensive lists and social performance 82–84
interactional theory 28
interactionism 32
Israel 14

Jefferson, T. 14

King, M. L., Jr. 14
KingJamesOnlineProject 43
Kinnaman, D. 98–99, 103

Lawrence, L. 17, 18
Lazarus 11
Lewis, B. 105
Lindbeck, G. 4, 42, 92
Liquid Scripture 7
Lovato, D. 81
Lövheim, M. 2–3, 35, 93, 109
Lynch, G. 109
Lyons, G. 99

Malley, B. 11, 17–18, 103
Marwick, A. 30
Mason, M. 95
McConnell, F. 6, 8, 11
McIntosh, E. 92, 108, 109
meaning-making process, faith as 99–100
media ecology 102–110
mediated presence of the Bible 9
mediatization of religion 3
Mendoza, M. 81–82
Meredith, C. 10
metaphysics 94, 95
microblogging, spiritual 23, 25, 32; *see also* Twitter
Milgram, S. 28
moralistic therapeutic deism (MTD) 17; "creed" of 93; growth of adoption of 92–102; limitations to 95–96; as live-out version of religion 102; media ecology and 106–107; metaphysics and 94, 95; in popular shared Bible verses 35–36, 42, 44, 78, 83–84, 85, 88; postmodernism and 94; as 'practice-based faith' 96–98; shift toward 92, 111–112; subjective turn and 96–97
Morgan, D. 109
multi-player online gaming 32
Murthy, D. 25, 28, 30, 33–34
Myles, R. 10
mysterium tremendum 95

nationalism, Christian 14, 15, 109–110
National Study of Youth and Religion 92
Network for New Media, Religion and Digital Culture Studies (NNMRDC) 25
network sociality 25, 26–27
Neuromancer 20

New York Times 24
Nikolev, D. 26
Noah 11
Noll, M. 15–16

Obama, B. 14
OpenBible 22, 43, 44, 45; analysis and reflection on shared verses 79–82
ordinary social performance of Bible engagement 4, 36–37, 79, 111
ordinary theology 3, 100

Pacquiao, M. 81
Paraclesis 8
Paraphrases 9
performance on social media 30–31, 34
performative belief 2, 35, 72, 85–86, 88, 93–95, 111
Perrin, R. 78–79, 111
personal branding 30
phatic communication 27
'photoshopped self' 28–29
pick and mix spirituality 102, 111
Poleg, E. 8, 10
postmodernism 94
practice-based faith 96–98, 101–102, 108
propositional belief 1–2, 4, 85, 88, 91–92, 108
Pyper, H. 10

Reagan, R. 13
Reformation, the 8, 96
Reimagining Bible Literacy 37
religion, mediatization of 3
Religion in Britain Since 1945 1
Rethinking Biblical Literacy 9–10, 12, 15
Richards, A. 82
rituals, microblogging 32
Rodman, R. 17
Rogers, R. 25
Rojek, C. 26, 27, 28, 31
Rowlands, C. 19

Schweitzer, F. 100–101
Second Life 24
secularization 13–14
'selfie dysmorphia' 29
self-representation on social media 24–25, 28–29

seven dimensions of belief 2–3
sharing, online 21, 29, 32–34
Sherwood, Y. 10
Siker, J. 7, 21–23, 70
Smith, C. 4, 17, 35–36, 71, 88, 92–93, 95, 97, 102, 110–111; *see also* moralistic therapeutic deism (MTD)
Smith, S. 22, 40
Social Life of Scripture, The 17
social media: anxiety and 30–31; banality on 27, 28; Bible tweets on 22–24, 105–106; changing faith due to new 102–110; community development on 24–25; Digital Religion and 25; engagement with, as performance 29–30, 34; as exhibition space 30, 31–32; 'liking' and 'sharing' of Bible texts on 21, 29, 32–34; network sociality on 25, 26–27; personal branding on 30; self-representation on 24–25, 28–29; spiritual microblogging on 23, 25; as synthetic situation 30; telepresence on 28; types of spiritual expression on 24; utterances on 27; *see also* Twitter
social performance of Bible engagement 4
social shaping of technology 3
Stokel-Walker, C. 103
Storm, I. 95
subjective turn 96–97
surveys and censuses 1
synthetic situation, social media as 30

Tebow, T. 81
telepresence 28
theocentric verses 36, 69, 75–80, 88, 93, 104, 111–112
Theological Action Research (TAR) 101–102
therapeutic commodity, religion as 94
Trump, D. 13
Turner, T. 71
Twitch 32
Twitter 22–24, 32, 102; celebrity culture on 80–82; Digital Millennials as primary user base of 38; as flat hierarchy 26; network sociality and 25, 26; as persuasive technology 105; sharing the Bible on 21, 29, 32–34;

worldwide reach and connectivity of 26; *see also* social media
'twitter of faith' 32

United Bible Society 43–44
United Kingdom, decline of Bible-centrism in the 11–12
United States, the: Bible engagement in 12–19; Christian nationalism in 14, 15, 109–110; Evangelical Christianity in 13–15; growth of adoption of MTD in 92–93; turn towards secularization in 13–14

Vásquez, M. 99
Virgil 6
vlogging 32
Voas, D. 95
von Bingen, H. 9

Ward, P. 100
Weaver, J. B. 32–33, 70
Whatsapp 32
Whitehead, A. 14
Woodhead, L. 4, 36, 42, 92, 93, 96
Word in Place: Reading the New Testament in Contemporary Contexts, The 17, 18–19
Wuthnow, R. 95

YouTube 22, 37
YouVersion 34, **43**, 43–45, 62, 63n4, 88, 102; analysis and reflection on shared verses 64–72, **65–67**; intensive lists and social performance 82–84; as persuasive technology 104–105

Zylstra, S. 68–69

For Product Safety Concerns and Information please contact our EU representative GPSR@taylorandfrancis.com
Taylor & Francis Verlag GmbH, Kaufingerstraße 24, 80331 München, Germany

www.ingramcontent.com/pod-product-compliance
Lightning Source LLC
Chambersburg PA
CBHW070738230426
43669CB00014B/2500